Milady's
Salon
Receptionist's
Handbook

Milady's Salon Receptionist's Handbook

Judy Ventura

Dudley Cosmetology University
Kernersville, North Carolina

Milady Publishing Company
(A Division of Delmar Publishers Inc.)

NOTICE TO THE READER

Publisher: Catherine Frangie
Developmental Editor: Joseph Miranda
Senior Project Editor: Laura Gulotty
Production Manager: John Mickelbank
Art/Design Supervisor: Susan Mathews
Freelance Project Editor: Pamela Fuller
Photographer: Michael A. Gallitelli
   On location at the Rielm Salon, Latham, N.Y., and at the Austin Beauty School, Albany, N.Y., with Dino Petrocelli
Cover Design: design M design W
Cover Photographs: Michael A. Gallitelli

Copyright © 1993
Milady Publishing Company
(A Division of Delmar Publishers Inc.)

Printed in the United States of America

10 9 8 7 6 5 4 3 2 1

Library of Congress Cataloging-in-Publication Data

Ventura, Judy.
   Milady's salon receptionist's handbook / Judy Ventura.
      p. cm.
   ISBN 1-56253-044-5
   1. Beauty shops—Employees. 2. Receptionists—Vocational guidance. I. Title.
TT958.V44 1993
651.3'743—dc20   93-3776
                                                                                              CIP

Dedication

This book is lovingly dedicated to my mother, Adeline Texeria.
Thank you for being a role model, my best friend, and the inspiration to succeed against all odds.

Contents

Preface

This training manual is written as a guide to prepare potential receptionists to efficiently and properly serve clients, staff, and management. It is primarily designed to provide readers with the material to learn proper reception procedures and techniques. While it is especially tailored for students who wish to become beauty salon receptionists, students who wish to become receptionists in any service-related business will also find useful information here.

The book has been prepared using the assumption that the material necessary for a course in receptionist training can be presented in seven two-hour classes. The seven chapters contained within offer a variety of topics that present a complete overview of this occupation, from how to make a great first impression to the receptionist's role in marketing and advertising.

Each chapter begins with measurable learning objectives that are discussed throughout the text and reinforced with review questions at the end. You will also find many examples of real-life salon situations, current trends, motivational tools, and industry statistics, making this book a complete learning experience and bridging the gap between the classroom and the workforce.

The author wishes to express her gratitude to Cathy Frangie and Sheila Furjanic of Milady Publishing Company for their continued support, guidance, and direction. Their professionalism and dedication have been invaluable.

Judy Ventura
Kernersville, North Carolina

Introduction

The receptionist is the first staff member a client talks to when calling or entering a beauty salon. A well-trained receptionist can greet clients, maintain salon culture, and promote business as well.

By learning basic phone skills, appointment procedures, and selling methods, the receptionist can serve as liaison between the salon staff and the client. The professional receptionist can handle client problems, staff concerns, and special needs that some clients may have.

Promoting the salon, helping with client records and inventory, and assisting the management may also be parts of the receptionist's job. Therefore the receptionist must acquire basic bookkeeping and record-keeping abilities.

The receptionist who successfully completes this course will be equipped to serve both staff and clients in a professional manner, earning an interesting career and lucrative income, as well as gaining the satisfaction and pride of being a well-trained, successful professional in the exciting beauty industry.

CHAPTER

1 How Important Is the Receptionist?

LEARNING OBJECTIVES

After completing this chapter, you should be able to:

❶ Recognize how important the receptionist is to the entire salon.

❷ List the ways in which the receptionist can make a great first impression.

❸ Describe a great working relationship between the salon owner (manager) and the receptionist.

❹ Explain how the receptionist can institute a pleasant, cordial, and professional atmosphere in the salon.

INTRODUCTION

This chapter is designed to help you realize the importance of the position you will hold when you become a well-trained receptionist.

The receptionist is the first and last contact the client has with the salon; therefore the impression you as a receptionist make on the client may set the tone for the entire appointment. (See Figure 1-1.)

From your first greeting on the phone to the way you escort the client to the door as he or she exits the salon, you will have the opportunity to either make the client feel welcomed, comfortable, and important, or as disposable as yesterday's newspaper.

Your responsibilities as a receptionist may differ, depending on the needs of the salon you are working in. The basic job

1

Figure 1-1 The receptionist is the first person a client comes in contact with at a salon. Greet the client with a smile, and project a positive image.

description for the receptionist, however, will give you a general idea of the type of work you will be expected to do.

The professional receptionist is required to greet clients, answer the phone, make appointments, sell retail items as well as salon services, coordinate salon schedules, cash out clients, keep records of salon business, and assist the owner with marketing and advertising.

Those skills can be learned, practiced, and mastered. The ingredients you should bring to this occupation are:

- A love for people (be a real "people person"),
- The ability to communicate effectively,
- The desire to make clients feel comfortable,
- A determination to work hard and succeed.

Although the demands on a good receptionist can be many, the rewards can equal them in number. A well-trained, professional receptionist can earn the respect of the owner, staff, and clients, as well as an above-average income.

How Important Is the Receptionist?

Consider this statistic: Studies show that 68 percent of the time customers leave a business, they do so because "somebody" offended them. Then think about how many important points of contact occur between the receptionist and the client. The receptionist is the first person from the salon who speaks with the client on the telephone, the first person who greets and welcomes the client into the salon, and the last person from the salon to say good-bye and invite the client to return. These points of contact all provide opportunities for the receptionist to cement the relationship with that client.

THE IMPRESSION THE RECEPTIONIST PROJECTS TO SALON CLIENTS

To become a successful salon receptionist, you must learn to project a professional image at all times. (See Figure 1-2.) You have the unique position to:

- Mediate (between client and operator),
- Motivate (staff morale as well as client sales),
- Navigate (traffic flow and salon sales),
- Initiate retail sales.

As a receptionist, you will be able to help a salon grow and prosper when you:

- Look professional,
- Act professional,
- Speak like a professional.

Figure 1-2 The successful salon receptionist must learn to project a professional image at all times.

Let's look at a situation where a receptionist is needed to "navigate" or "steer" the flow of clients in this busy salon.

The phone rings in the salon. A new client is calling to make an appointment for a consultation. Although the client has never been to this salon before, she has heard how talented the staff is, and in fact they are so talented that they stay booked up at all times. (Booked up means that there are no available appointments, because clients have scheduled appointments for all the hours the salon is open.)

Today in particular the staff is so busy that no one is able to get to the phone while it is ringing, and the call goes unanswered! The potential new client hangs up and calls another salon to schedule an appointment.

That same day, Mrs. Texiera, a longstanding client of the salon, stands at the reception desk for a very long time. Every staff member is so busy that they are unable to leave their clients and help Mrs. Texiera choose her retail purchases and book another appointment. So Mrs. Texiera plunks down her money and sales check and leaves the salon without her favorite hairspray, nail polish, and shampoo. On the way home, she stops at a drugstore for the items she had planned to purchase in the salon.

This salon may be the busiest in town, but it may never reach its full financial potential. Although the owner has spared no expense in decor, staffing of stylists, and providing state-of-the-art services and products, the salon will have trouble retaining clients who find that they can't:

- Purchase products easily,
- Make an appointment when it is convenient to call the salon,
- Receive a pleasant smile as they walk in the door,
- Feel appreciated as they leave the salon.

What this salon needs is a professional receptionist!

Clients who are prepared to visit an upscale salon and spend their money generously on services and retail products expect flawless service and a great deal of personal attention. (Upscale salons are exclusive and provide more luxurious services and atmosphere than a budget or value-oriented salon.) The presence of a receptionist implies that this salon's foremost concern is the client's needs and desires.

Figure 1-3 A well-trained receptionist will bring more revenue to the salon by acting as a salesperson.

In addition, a well-trained receptionist can bring the salon more business and sell products that only the receptionist will have time to demonstrate or promote. (See Figure 1-3.)

Let's look at this same salon, after they hire a professional receptionist:

> The phone rings, and the receptionist answers with a smile in her voice. "Good morning! Ventura's Unique Salon— how may I help you? Oh, I see, you're a new client, and you would like to make an appointment for a consultation? . . . We would love to serve you. We can take you at 2:00 on Tuesday, if that's convenient for you. It is a good time? Fine! I've booked you for Tuesday, the 25th, at 2:00. And, Mrs. Texiera, may I suggest that you arrive a few moments early to allow time to browse through our new style books?" (Meanwhile, Mrs. Rowlett walks up to the desk and is ready to check out.) The receptionist smiles and winks at Mrs. Rowlett and motions by lifting her index finger that it will only be a moment, hands Mrs. Rowlett a perfume sample, finishes her phone call, and her conversation now centers around Mrs. Rowlett. It sounds something like this: "Mrs. Rowlett, you look great in the new style we found in the style book. I love the golden highlights you decided to try. I have the perfect nail polish to accent that new color, and here's the shampoo you will need to take care of your color-treated hair and keep the color from fading too soon! And how do you like that new perfume? Isn't it a light spring fragrance? Doesn't it remind you of a field of flowers? Would you like to try the cologne, spray, or sachet form?"

Are you beginning to see the difference that a well-trained, professional receptionist can make? The salon that was too busy to give clients personal attention is now projecting an image that confirms

- We care about you.
- We want your business.
- We will take all the time needed to properly serve you.
- We hope to make you feel as great as we make you look.
- We are listening to your concerns and desires.

The receptionist is a vital part of the salon team. The time and attention the client receives from the receptionist can increase business immeasurably!

Beyond the Desk: Career Opportunities

In case you think that as a receptionist you will spend all of your days behind the desk on the phone, you will be interested to learn about the variety of service-oriented career opportunities available in the beauty salon for you. Chances are, if you work in a smaller salon, your job will encompass all of these duties. Working in a larger salon gives you the opportunity to specialize.

- Hostess: At Hair Benders, a full service salon in Altamonte Springs, California, owner Candi Ekstrom employs a "hostess." Similar to that position in many restaurants, the hostess greets every client and gives new clients a tour of the salon, introduces them to Candi, introduces them to the staff members they will be seeing, and takes whatever steps are necessary to make the new client feel welcome in the large salon. The hostess also serves refreshments to clients throughout the salon. At the end of the visit, she asks clients how they felt about their salon experience, how they enjoyed her as a hostess, and lets them know how much the staff appreciates their continued business.
- Telemarketer: At Charles Penzone's The Grand Salon in Columbus, Ohio, a staff of telemarketers answers phones, returns calls, rebooks clients, and handles a variety of special products for the salon manager.
- Tour guide: At Van Michael salon in Atlanta, new clients receive a tour of every inch of the salon from the coat room to the area where they receive complimentary makeup services.

- Customer service representative: At The Grand Salon, one receptionist guides clients who have purchased spa packages from one station to the next. This staff member also orders breakfasts and lunches for clients and continuously talks up the salon/spa and its offerings throughout the day.
- Retail product manager: At Eric Fisher salon in Wichita, Kansas, the staff includes a part-time retail product manager who stocks shelves and keeps products neatly arranged. At other salons this job is expanded to include product ordering and inventory control.

HOW TO MAKE A GREAT FIRST IMPRESSION

The dictionary defines the word *impression* as an effect produced on the mind, an *imprint*.

Every time the salon door opens and a client steps inside, you make an impression. Every time you answer the phone, you make your imprint on a potential client. The question you must continually ask yourself is: Am I making the best impression I can make, on every client I come in contact with?

You, as a professional receptionist, must be sure to make every client feel welcome and important, immediately. You cannot change a bad first impression. You only have one opportunity to make the client like you. Once you have made your mark, it will be difficult to reverse the opinion the client has of you. No matter how tired you are, or how badly you feel, you must smile at every client and be cheerful in every phone call you answer! A client who happens to walk in the door when you are not well, overly busy, or upset deserves the same good service and cheerful attitude as the first client of the day. Treat each client as if the salon has no other clients, because all clients are individuals with individual needs, wants, and desires.

The best way to make a good impression on clients is to truly care about people and enjoy working with them. Did you ever meet someone who truly loves being around people? This type of individual is called a "people person." Some characteristics of a people person are:

- Happy attitude,
- Always smiling,
- Finds goodness in everyone,

- Freely compliments others,
- Is optimistic (always sees the bright side),
- Is charismatic (people are drawn to them).

A people person attracts other people like a magnet attracts metal. Everyone enjoys being around a people person. The receptionist who has good people skills can survive a client calling to change an appointment four times and still be pleasant enough to serve that client the next time he or she calls. The receptionist with great people skills can knock over a display just as you walk in the salon door and end up selling you an item from that display!

A people person can become the perfect receptionist, because a people person realizes that every disadvantage has an opposite and equal advantage.

The professional receptionist knows that the way to open the client's purse strings is through the receptionist's own personality. A happy person, with a positive attitude and the ability to make a good first impression, is bound to succeed in retail sales as well as in reception duties.

Let's look at two examples of first impressions.

Example 1

Mary has been the receptionist for a year. She is accurate with appointments and cashiering, but her first impressions are a little off! Her appearance is never tidy, her hair, nails, and makeup are not always freshly done, and she spends too much time on the phone with friends. She is polite, but not overly helpful. Although she is never rude to clients, she would never go out of her way to accommodate a client's special needs. It would never occur to Mary to suggest additional services to clients or help them choose new styles or products to use at home. Mary is accurate, but does not possess the "people skills" needed to be an outstanding receptionist.

Example 2

Gina is the receptionist in the salon across the street. Her hair and makeup are always done to perfection, and her nails are perfectly manicured. She usually wears the latest styles the salon is promoting in hair color and cuts. Gina has a beautiful smile that you can almost hear on the telephone. Gina also spends quality time with every client and always tries to be very patient with client concerns. She is as helpful on the phone as she is in person. Clients in this salon feel comfortable and relaxed, secure in the knowledge that their needs are Gina's first and foremost concern. Gina is great at first impressions; she practices making clients feel welcomed the moment they arrive in the salon. She is relaxed and happy serving clients, and the flow of clients is reflective of her happy and positive attitude. She is a real people person and a super receptionist. The manager, stylists, and clients all depend on Gina. She knows the secret of being a great receptionist is to treat each client as though he or she is the only client you have. Being great at first impressions, like Gina, is an important attribute for any receptionist, because you never get a second chance to make a first impression!

The Right Stuff

What does it take to be a great receptionist? Some of the basics are explained in this chapter. According to the owners of some of the top salons in the country, here are some of the characteristics that really make a receptionist stand out:

- **Adaptability.** One salon owner put it this way: "The best receptionist knows how to be mature—one year older than the person he or she is dealing with."
- **Empathy.** The ideal receptionist understands how to stand in the client's shoes.
- **Responsibility.** Owners and managers rely on top receptionists to run the front desk and oversee the staff in their absence.
- **Motivation.** Even when the salon is not too busy, the receptionist can never spend enough time catering to clients—without being reminded.
- **Taste.** The winning image is fashionable, neutral, non-threatening, and gives clients the impression that they would not mind "being in the same space." Remember, the client will form a first impression of you within 30 seconds.

YOUR RELATIONSHIP WITH MANAGEMENT

The relationship that the receptionist has with management is a crucial one! Managers and owners must treat the receptionist well if they expect the receptionist to do a great job. An unhappy

Figure 1-4 A salon manager and a receptionist must communicate about products and styles.

receptionist cannot be upbeat and cheerful to clients. By the same token, the receptionist is expected to give unquestioning loyalty and commitment to the salon staff and clients. (See Figure 1-4.)

The manager and the receptionist must be able to:

- Communicate,
- Work well as a team,
- Respect each other's opinions,
- Motivate the staff,
- Recognize and serve client needs,
- Maintain a successful retail program.

When searching for the perfect receptionist, a manager will seek persons with these qualities (see Figure 1-5):

- Even temper,
- Patience,
- Pleasant speaking voice,
- Ability to make quick decisions,
- Desire to sell products,
- Ability to promote salon and staff,
- Impeccable appearance,
- Loyalty,

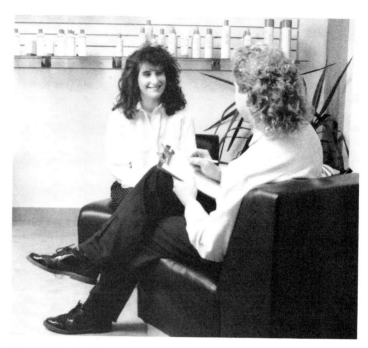

Figure 1-5   A salon manager will look for certain qualities when interviewing a prospective receptionist.

- Honesty,
- Dependability,
- Stable work record.

If you become an efficient receptionist, you will be well paid. Receptionists are usually paid a salary, and some receptionists are paid a commission on retail sales. You may also enjoy free services as part of your benefit package. A receptionist who receives free services will be a walking advertisement for the salon. There is no better way to promote a new service than to have the receptionist wear it! Whether or not you receive free services, you must be sure that your hair, makeup, and nails are always impeccable and that the clothes you wear are businesslike.

Loyalty is one of the most essential requirements for a receptionist. Management will expect the receptionist to be loyal to the salon, the staff, and the clients.

Management will also expect the receptionist to be prepared to help the salon staff make clients comfortable. (See Figure 1-6.) This may include

Figure 1-6 A receptionist should be prepared to help the salon staff, like matching a stylist with a new client.

- Assisting with schedules,
- Relaying messages between phone clients and staff,
- Matching stylists and new clients,
- Directing the flow of traffic (clients) in the salon,
- Assisting clients with special needs.

Today, more than ever, many special clients will need special attention from a receptionist. (See Figure 1-7.) For example:

- Handicapped clients,
- Developmentally disabled clients,
- Clients with sight or hearing impairments,
- Older people,
- Persons using English as a second language,
- Children.

Management may occasionally require the receptionist to perform tasks that are not part of the routine job description. This could include setting up a display, running an emergency errand, or even helping fold towels if the entire staff is too busy to fold them! Managers may ask you to be a good team member and help out on occasions when there is an emergency or the

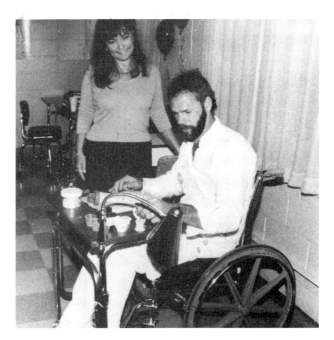

Figure 1-7 A receptionist assisting a client in a wheelchair.

staff is overly busy. (See Figure 1-8.) Sometimes being part of a team means doing tasks that are not pleasant, but are necessary for the welfare and comfort of the client and the entire salon. Whenever you can, try to be as helpful as you can. If a special request seems unreasonable to you, discuss it with your manager. You should be able to communicate with the manager on an open and frank level. If there is a challenge, or even a concern or a misunderstanding, they must be able to

- Discuss the issue, calmly,
- Be open and honest,
- Be ready to compromise,
- Have an understanding and forgiving nature.

Managers must be ready to spend time explaining job descriptions and duties to the receptionist. Wages and benefits should be discussed and described in writing. A receptionist who knows what is expected and what the compensation is will be relaxed and able to do a better job.

Often a receptionist will be more aware of the salon challenges than the manager. This is because the receptionist is with the

Figure 1-8 Being a good team member is essential to good salon management.

staff and clients at all times; a rapport develops—a relationship that helps communication. At times the receptionist will hear confidential information from both staff and clientele. The receptionist should never violate anyone's confidence and betray a trust. It is unforgivable to be untrustworthy, and you could lose your job if you betray a confidence. Also, don't allow the staff to burden you with personal problems—refer them to the manager. Never participate in gossip in the salon, and never side with the staff members against each other or management. (See Figure 1-9.) Try to

Figure 1-9 Never participate in gossip in the salon.

remain neutral if possible. Never discuss paychecks, income, or salon business with staff—refer them to the manager. Management expects you, as the receptionist, to keep privileged information confidential. Management will soon recognize your professional reception skills, and you will earn a place of respect and importance in the salon. As you become the right hand to management, staff and clients will begin to find you indispensable too!

Selecting the Owner Who's Right for You

The relationship between the receptionist and the salon owner affects how you feel about your work experience. In many salons the atmosphere takes on the personality of the owner. You can sense this when you first walk into the salon for your interview. Do you feel a sense of warmth? Are you shown around the salon? Do the staff members seem warm and welcoming? Does the salon feel like it's an environment you would like to become a part of? If you answer "yes" to all of these questions, proceed with the interview. If you answer "no" to two or more, you might want to reconsider whether this salon is a place where you want to spend at least eight hours a day.

MAINTAINING SALON CULTURE

It has often been said that a picture is worth a thousand words. This is particularly true for the image you, the receptionist, create for every client. You set the tone for the entire salon. If you paint a beautiful picture for the client, he or she will be ready for services the staff is ready to provide. Your reception area must greet every client by being

- Neat and organized,
- Decorated nicely,
- Well stocked with retail items,
- Clean,
- Efficient.

You must keep the waiting area and retail displays impeccably clean and organized. Magazines must be current and in good

Figure 1-10 The receptionist should keep the salon waiting area clean and organized.

shape. Throw out tattered magazines, and keep the material varied and interesting. (See Figure 1-10.) The coffee table must be kept clear of old cups, and ashtrays must be kept clean. All trash should be cleared immediately. Retail items should never be dusty. Rotate stock, and discard items with expired dates for fresh sale. (See Figure 1-11.)

You should always arrive at work at least fifteen minutes earlier than the first appointment, in order to prepare the waiting

Figure 1-11 Retail items should be kept ordered and current.

area, displays, and yourself to greet the client properly. Be ready to smile and greet clients, even if they arrive early for appointments. Your hair, nails, and appearance should be fresh, your clothes professional, and your speech should always be polite. To avoid misunderstandings, always use proper speech—avoid using slang. Never curse or use profanity on the job. Practice your professional behavior and reception techniques on family, friends, and salon staff. Ask them for an honest critique, and then learn from their suggestions. Your personal hygiene must be impeccable. Sweet breath is a must. Avoid foods like garlic and onions while working. Keep mouthwash handy and a toothbrush in your purse.

How to Project the Wrong Image

- Overdoing it: Wearing too much makeup, wild hair, or clothes that are more cutting edge than most of the salon's clients. When in doubt, less is truly best.
- Over accessorizing: A refined, professional image calls for few but striking accessories.
- Foregoing makeup altogether: A receptionist is a beauty professional and projects the image that the salon is selling.
- Avoid "dragon" nails: Nails need a professional touch too. Keep them well groomed, professional, and polished, but not overdone.

Be cordial to every client, even those who aren't particularly nice. You never know what happened to Ms. Jones on her way here. Perhaps a traffic tieup or a sick child are making her upset today. Perhaps your pleasant smile will make the client feel better. Besides, other clients are watching you serve Ms. Jones, and they are forming an opinion of you too! Clients will automatically assume that you represent the staff, and they will expect the entire salon to treat them as you do. This is an awesome responsibility. You can't afford to have a bad day, or even a bad hour. If you turn off a potential client, or offend a current client, you could affect the salon's income, or even lose a client! You not only have the responsibility to maintain the salon's culture, you, as the receptionist, will be the salon's culture.

REVIEW QUESTIONS

1. What type of image should the receptionist always have?
2. What does the mere presence of a receptionist reveal to clients?
3. Why should the receptionist be concerned with first impressions?
4. What are some ways the receptionist can maintain salon culture?
5. Write a 200-word essay that tells why you want to become a receptionist and what rewards you expect from this career.

C H A P T E R

2 The Phone Command Center

LEARNING OBJECTIVES

After completing this chapter, you should be able to:

❶ Recognize the importance of a good phone personality.
❷ Be able to book appointments over the phone.
❸ Be able to turn phone cancellations into an appointment.
❹ Sell additional services over the phone.
❺ Sell retail items over the phone.
❻ Create interest in salon promotions over the phone.

INTRODUCTION

One of the most critical areas of salon service is the technique of properly handling the phone in a busy salon. (See Figure 2-1.) As a professional receptionist, you will be required to develop a phone personality that is

- Pleasant,
- Patient,
- Helpful,
- Exciting and enthusiastic.

The impression that you make on every client who calls the salon is the first impression that clients will have of the entire salon! You may never have a second chance to make up for a mistaken phone impression. If you seem aloof, too busy, uncaring, or impolite, the client may have second thoughts about keeping the appointment. You should answer every phone call as though you were expecting someone to tell you

Figure 2-1 A good phone personality is a must for a successful receptionist.

that you just won a million dollar sweepstakes. Above all else, every time you answer the phone, smile! A smile on your face will be evident in your voice and will start you on the road to being pleasant to all clients! Some of your phone duties may be

- Making appointments,
- Changing existing appointments,
- Reminding clients of their appointments,
- Answering client questions and concerns,
- Taking messages for the staff,
- Informing clients of special offers,
- Placing phone orders for supplies.

Your phone duties will be dictated by the type of salon you work in and how busy the staff is. Your primary phone duty is to make a good impression.

 Putting Personal Phone Calls on Hold

Problem: While working the front desk, you find that Cindy, a busy stylist, receives up to five personal phone calls a day from her boyfriend and other friends. She often leaves her clients to take these calls and can stay on the line for more than five minutes while her client waits and your line is tied up. How can you handle this situation?

Solution: When these calls come through and Cindy is with a client, politely ask the caller if you can take a message and inform the caller that you will give the message to Cindy as soon as she is free. Be insistent if you have established that the call is not an emergency. Make sure that you do give the message to Cindy as soon as she is between clients. If she tries to return the call, politely remind her that the desk phone is for incoming calls from clients and refer her to the line in the employee break room. If the situation persists or if your salon has a written policy on personal calls that is being broken, you might need to bring the situation to the attention of your salon manager.

Another solution might be to bring the situation to your manager in a general sense, without mentioning names, and suggest that you review telephone policies at your next staff meeting. That way you can remind Cindy about the meeting if the situation occurs again. Some salons have installed pay phones for staff members to use to return calls during their established breaks.

DEVELOPING A PHONE PERSONALITY

The reception desk should always be quiet and organized. It should be removed from the hustle and bustle of the salon. You may not be able to hear phone clients properly if there is a blow dryer going next to you. If you are unable to hear the client well, you may confuse an appointment time and make a mistake that is costly to the salon. Therefore the reception desk and telephone should be in a quiet corner of the salon, where noise will not prevent proper phone reception.

If you are unable to clearly hear clients, a small, inexpensive attachment can be added to the phone to raise the volume when needed. Discuss this and any other special needs with management.

Checking Your Phone Voice

If you're new to the telephone—in a professional sense—you might want to check your phone voice to make sure it sounds as pleasing as possible. One good way is to practice speaking into a tape recorder. You might even want to hold the telephone in one hand and the tape recorder in the other to give you the sense of talking on the phone.

When you replay the recording, check the following:

- Is there a smile in your voice?
- Are you speaking clearly?
- Are you speaking slowly?
- Do you sound helpful?
- Do you sound interested in your work?
- Do you appear to be interested in every word the client is saying?

Replay the recording immediately, then put it away for several days. Replay it again to double check your "first" impression. You might want to have your salon manager or owner listen to your tape and critique it. Another good way to practice your telephone voice is to role play telephone situations with your manager or other staff members until you feel comfortable.

Always speak slowly and clearly when addressing clients on the phone. Avoid using slang terms, and always repeat the time and date of the appointment before ending the conversation. This will help eliminate misunderstandings in appointment times.

Be bright and cheerful, but avoid becoming overly involved in a conversation that could tie up the phone lines and keep other clients from getting through. Some salons may have call waiting or two phone lines; you will be able to switch from the first call to the second and ask each client to hold a moment as you recognize each client and their needs. Always keep the conversation light and professional, cheerful and brief, and remember to smile.

Before answering the phone in a busy salon, always take a moment to take a deep breath and relax, put on your smile, and then answer the phone. This is particularly important if you are hurried, tired, or just finished with a difficult client. (See Figure 2-2.) Remember, when the phone rings,

- PAUSE
- INHALE
- EXHALE
- SMILE

Then answer the phone! This is the P-I-E-S formula. A receptionist who does not take a moment to regroup between calls may make a mistake or give a mistaken impression on the phone. Use

Figure 2-2 In a busy salon atmosphere, the receptionist must be professional, cheerful, and accurate.

the P-I-E-S formula every time you answer the phone. Place the letters P-I-E-S on or next to the phone to remind you with every phone call you answer!

Always answer the phone by using the salon's name after a greeting; then offer to help the client.

> Example: Good morning! Michael's Salon; may I help you?
> or: Good afternoon, Beauty Boutique; may I make an appointment for you?

The management may want you to use another phrase to answer the phone, especially during a sale or a special promotion for holidays.

> Example: Merry Christmas, Sheri's Salon; may I help you?
> or: Happy holidays from Chuck's Salon, where perms are always our special.
> or: Thanks for calling Benjamin's Salon at Cornwallis Square; we are now open till 9, every night. May I help you?

Speak slowly and clearly so that clients can understand the message you are trying to convey.

TAKING AN APPOINTMENT/CANCELLATION OVER THE PHONE

Clients are not always able to keep an appointment made in advance, nor are they always able to make appointments in person. Therefore, you will be required to book appointments over the phone. Booking an appointment requires you to arrange for and record the correct time and date, stylist, and service for the client. (See Figure 2-3.) In Chapter 3 you will learn to determine the time needed for each service and how to write the appointment in the book. For now we will deal with the actual phone call arranging the appointment. Making a phone appointment may sound similar to this:

> Rinnng.
> P-I-E-S (Remember? Pause, inhale, exhale, smile.) Good morning, Chuck's Salon; may I help you?
> Yes, I can make that appointment for you. Ten o'clock Friday? That will be fine, Mr. Boudreau. Cheryl can take you at ten on Friday, the tenth of June, for a perm and cut. Can I make an appointment for a manicure at the same time? Great, we'll see you Friday at ten.

Figure 2-3 A receptionist is required to book appointments over the phone.

All of the elements of an appointment are important. Notice that the above example shows:

- How to answer the phone.
- How to take and confirm a time, date, and service.
- How to suggest an additional service.
- How to politely greet the phone client.
- How to properly end the phone conversation.
- How to include the stylist's name.

 ### Hold It! Putting Clients on Hold Must Be Handled Carefully

Your salon's front desk should have a procedure for putting clients on hold. It's best to avoid simply saying "Hold please" and then clicking the client out without asking for the client's permission. Here is one format to try:

Receptionist: Thank you for calling. Could you hold a moment, please?
(Wait for a response)
If yes, say, "Thank you."
If no, say, "How may I help you?"
When returning to a holding caller after no longer than 30 seconds, "Thank you for waiting. Susan speaking. How may I help you?"

Never allow a client to remain on hold for more than 30 seconds. If several lines are busy, move back and forth between the lines as needed. Use your best professional judgment, and keep the feelings of all clients in mind. Remember, the client standing in front of you can see how busy you are; the client put on hold automatically assumes you are goofing off.

Some clients may call to change or cancel appointments. It will be your responsibility as the receptionist to turn client objections into a new appointment. The following example shows one way of helping a client feel more secure, therefore rescheduling an appointment instead of canceling entirely.

Rinnng.
P-I-E-S
Happy Easter, G.M.T. Salon; may I help you? Oh, Ms. Turchetta, How are you? Afraid to have another perm? Your hair never looks the same when you do it as when the stylist does it, so you want to cancel your appointment? I have a suggestion for

you, Mrs. Turchetta. We hold a "care for your perm class" every Tuesday night. Many people have the same concerns about styling their new perms once they leave the salon. How about taking this week's class, as well as letting me schedule a new appointment for you after you have been to the class and are feeling better about the perm? The class is at 7 P.M., Tuesday. And how about a new hair appointment for a week from today, Wednesday the 15th, at 10 A.M.? Great; see you then.

Notice that the client's concerns about looking good after a new perm were addressed, and the client not only chose to keep her appointment on another day, but she will attend the class too! The receptionist greeted the client properly, repeated the date and time, and ended the conversation on a positive note. The client is now reassured, and the receptionist helped retain a client for the stylist and the salon.

With a little practice you will be able to help clients feel good about keeping their appointments. Be pleasant, courteous, and keep the client's best interests in mind, and she will sense that you are genuinely interested and want to help her!

Booking Appointments Via Phone

When booking appointments over the phone, asking several important questions can help you function as efficiently as possible. Try using this checklist:

- Ask the client if he or she has been to the salon before. If yes, you know the client will be familiar with your procedures. If no, then you will want to ask the client to arrive several minutes early to fill out the new client form and tour the salon.
- Ask if the client is requesting a specific stylist. Often the client on the phone assumes that you know who the regular stylist is. Asking avoids confusion when the client arrives.
- Ask if the client prefers early or late in the week and a morning or afternoon appointment. Then offer two time periods, beginning with your slowest times.
- If the client does not want either time, ask specifically when he or she would like to come in.
- Always repeat the day and time at the end of the conversation to confirm that you have the same understanding.

- If you can't agree on a time, ask the client if you can add her to your cancellation list and call her at the last minute if her desired time becomes free.

SELLING ON THE PHONE

You, as the receptionist, will be able to create interest in new services and products by discussing new items and promotions on the phone, as clients call in to make appointments.

To sell services on the phone, you must:

- Be aware of all the products and services the salon offers,
- Understand how each product and service benefits the client,
- Use the product or service yourself, or have firsthand knowledge or observation of the results available,
- Be aware of possible client concerns and objections and be informed enough to calm any concerns,
- Know which stylist offers each service,
- Know which retail items will help clients with a particular problem or need,
- Know how much time a service will take to complete.

The salon management must meet with you and explain each service offered, the results achieved, the cost of the service, and the time needed to perform this service. Likewise, management should explain every retail item and when to recommend it. Ask questions and take notes. Perhaps you will even be able to observe salon operations for a day or two before you begin your job as receptionist. Product manufacturers may supply the salon with retail product knowledge, booklets, and pamphlets. The more information you have about the product, the more often you will recommend it and sell it. At the very least, you should read the label on the products and note:

- Which products are for oily hair (scalp)?
- Which are for dry hair?
- Which are for tinted hair?
- Which are for sensitive skin?
- What warnings are on the label? Who should not use this product?
- Which staff members like and recommend this product? why?

Make a list of salon services and which staff members perform these services. Ask the stylists how long it takes to perform each service, what the cost is, and who can or cannot have each particular service. Ask questions and ask to see pictures if you don't understand. Until you have a clear understanding you will not be able to correctly sell services to clients, and you will not book appointments properly.

Build New Staff Members Over the Phone!

The phone can be a great tool to build tickets and build the clientele of your newest staff member before the client even arrives. The advantages? The client knows in advance that she will be spending extra time at the salon, and she will be looking forward to the additional services as soon as she walks in the door.

Here's how it works: When the client calls, ask her when she would like to come in; then say, "Mrs. Kelly, I have good news. Bob's Salon has a new nail technician named Janice. She is very good and would love to offer her services to you. She has some free time after your haircut. Would you like me to book a manicure for you too? You've been working so hard, you really deserve the extra treat."

Chances are, Mrs. Kelly will immediately say, "Oh, I really need a manicure. That would be lovely." Or, she will ask you how much extra it will cost. If Janice has very few regulars yet, she might want to offer the service to regular salon clients either half off or on a complimentary basis when the client purchases a salon service at regular price. That way, she can get to know the salon's clients without spending extra dollars on advertising to attract new clients from outside. The client gets a great service, which she will probably book again at regular price. And Janice will have the chance to sell retail nail products to make up the difference. Everyone wins!

The same conversation works for a new esthetician, makeup artist, color specialist, or masseuse.

If you are informed, pleasant, and polite, you will always be able to sell additional services and products on the phone. Be honest, and only suggest services and products when you sincerely believe that the client will benefit from them. A sincere effort to help the client will bring a sure sale!

Always mention promotions on the phone. Before you end a phone conversation, mention the upcoming cut-a-thon for charity, or the perm sale beginning next week. An example of this might be:

> Rinnng.
> P-I-E-S
> Good morning, Adam's Salon. Hello, Mr. Christopher, you would like an appointment for a manicure today? Yes, we can take you at two this afternoon. Oh, did I mention that we have a perm sale this week? I remember we talked about the fullness that a perm would give your hair. Wouldn't this be a great time to try one? And guess what? I have that new after-shave you were asking about; I am holding one aside for you. Great, we'll see you at two for a manicure and a perm. Mary can take you for the perm at the same time as your manicure is done. See you at two!

This receptionist made a service sale (perm) and a retail sale (after-shave) because she took the time to remember what the client wanted and asked about on his last visit to the salon. Sales are a transference of feelings, and this receptionist transferred the feelings of excitement about the perm sale and after-shave to the client. The client then developed a need or desire for the items. Remember, selling is a transference of your feelings! Get excited about your job, the services you sell, and the products available in your salon.

REVIEW QUESTIONS

1. The telephone area in the salon is known as the _____ center.
2. Clients may call to _____ or _____ appointments.
3. What must the receptionist know about a product before she can sell it?
4. Selling is a transference of _____.
5. What are some ways to turn client concerns into additional services?

3 Scheduling

LEARNING OBJECTIVES

After completing this chapter, you should be able to:

❶ Understand the importance of proper scheduling of clients and services.

❷ Be able to set up and maintain an appointment book.

❸ Schedule personnel to accommodate busy salon times.

❹ Coordinate staff schedules and client appointments.

INTRODUCTION

Scheduling clients and coordinating appointments with staff schedules is a very important part of the receptionist's job. The receptionist is usually the best judge of the flow of clients and which times of the day or week are the most requested times, as well as which services are being requested most often.

Salon staff members who wish to build up their clientele base and managers who desire to accommodate client needs will depend on the receptionist's opinion to set up salon schedules and coordinate appointments and schedules.

It is essential that the receptionist become familiar with appointment book procedures, as well as how to estimate the amount of time needed to perform each service.

COORDINATING PERSONNEL SCHEDULES AND BUSY SALON TIMES

Scheduling appointments for salon clients is a large part of a receptionist's responsibilities. The appointment book helps plan

DAY _Thursday_ DATE _6/29_ 19._90_

OPER.	Cathy (STYLIST)	Jacquie (STYLIST)	Marie (STYLIST)	Lucille (STYLIST)	Joey (MANICURE)	Dorothy (WAXING)	OPER.
8:00							8:00
8:15							8:15
8:30							8:30
8:45							8:45
9:00		Carol Gianni cut 555- blowdry 1874		Ellen Adrupaz hair 555- color 2431 trim			9:00
9:15							9:15
9:30	Susan White Shampoo 555-		Telma Brooks shampoo 555- set 5668		Merry Moran basic 555- 3396	Abigail Spiegel full 555- leg 2940	9:30
9:45					Sherri Salem		9:45
10:00	cut 1561	Linda Klein braid 555- 4166			tips 555- wraps 7647	bikini	10:00
10:15							10:15
10:30	Peggy Neill hair 555-		Catherine Bass blowdry 555- 8370	Annie Rolland Shampoo 555- set 9420		Jude Preston full 555- 6324	10:30
10:45						leg	10:45
11:00	Color 9853		Sally McFadden perm 555- 2993		Lisa Tesar basic 555- 3010	Pat Keller	11:00
11:15						lip/brow 555- 0179	11:15
11:30	Barb Matthews cut blowdry 555- 7207	Heidi Blau hair 555- color 8129		Jill Brevda cut blowdry 555- 3332	Neil Sprock french 555- 8334	Sue Axelrod	11:30
11:45						full 555-	11:45
12:00				Matt Reagan beard 555- trim 1300		leg 4012 bikini	12:00
12:15							12:15
12:30	Kyle Harmon perm 555-		Laura DeFlora perm 555- trim 3276		Elisa Klein basic 555- 2817		12:30
12:45							12:45
1:00	trim 1734	Rich Weller perm 555-		Ruth Edison perm 555-	Jim Stein basic 555- 8273	Laura Louie bikini 555- 5107	1:00
1:15				trim 2705			1:15
1:30		8163	Claire Sweet cut blowdry 555- 4278		Nancy Goldberg french 555- 1779	Denise Carlson arm 555- 4461	1:30
1:45							1:45
2:00	Allison Nortier Shampoo 555- cut 0127			Yolanda Brown cut 555- blowdry 2576		Kendra Miller full 555- 2704	2:00
2:15							2:15
2:30	Jennifer Banko hair 555- 1320	Liz Collito braid 555- 2703			Linda Douglas tips 555- wraps 1724	leg	2:30
2:45							2:45
3:00	Color		Liz Daley perm 555- 2058	Lori Amsdell hair 555-		Beth Meadows lip/brow 555- 7190	3:00
3:15						bikini	3:15
3:30			trim	Color 1453	Brenda Turner		3:30
3:45	Ginny Chamberlain Shampoo 555- 4673				tips 555- wraps 0039	Tracy Brost	3:45
4:00						bikini 555- 3212	4:00
4:15							4:15
4:30	Mary Porter cut blowdry 555- 2862	Anne Thompson perm 555- trim 1117		Elaine Zantos cut blowdry 555- 2873		Jasmine Fine lip/brow 555- 3623	4:30
4:45							4:45
5:00			Mary Gallagher cut blowdry 555- 9612	Joe Miranda beard 555- trim 4800	Shelli Dills french 555- 4726		5:00
5:15							5:15
5:30			Pam Jeffries hair 555- color 8720				5:30
5:45	Taryn Liebl perm 555- 2878				Jacquie Flynn tips 555- wraps 8047		5:45
6:00							6:00
6:15							6:15

Figure 3-1 An appointment book schedule.

and keep a record of the clients served on a particular day. (See Figure 3-1.)

The appointment book shows what is actually taking place in the salon. It lists the stylists and the date, time, and year at the top of the page. Under each stylist's name is a place to write appointments. Note the times at the sides of the page, which coordinate with each line of the book. The time lines are broken down into 15-minute increments, so you can book appointments on the hour, half hour, or quarter hour.

Using an appointment book helps the salon arrange for appointments for each staff member, at times that meet clients' needs. For example, Cathy works from 9:30 A.M. to 8 P.M. on Thursdays. Mrs. Susan White called to schedule an appointment for a haircut at 9:30 on Thursday, the 29th, with Cathy. It would be the receptionist's responsibility to write this appointment in the correct space, on the correct page of the appointment book. After checking the page to find the correct day and date, you would look under Cathy's column and determine whether she could take Mrs. White at 9:30 A.M. If Cathy is not scheduled to work on that day or at that hour, or if Cathy already has an appointment at that time, the receptionist would either suggest another time when Cathy is free to take the client or another stylist to help the client.

If Cathy is usually busy at this time, or several clients have requested Cathy on her day off, yet Cathy is never busy on Tuesdays, you may need to keep a record of clients you were unable to book with Cathy and give this information to the manager. The manager will probably suggest to Cathy that she change her day off to accommodate her clients' needs, and help Cathy stay busier and earn more money. Therefore, the receptionist not only books appointments, she helps the salon make efficient use of time.

Another example would be if Ms. Heidi Blau calls for an appointment with Cathy on the same day, but can only come in on her lunch hour, which is at 11:30. Cathy is already booked at this time, but Heidi has to have her hair color done that day because she is leaving town on a last minute trip. The receptionist suggests another stylist, Jackie, who is available to serve her at that time, and Cathy will be there to assist with formulas and special needs or concerns. The receptionist is able to help the client and keep the business in the salon. If the receptionist had not suggested another stylist, the client might have chosen to try another salon in this emergency situation.

Controlling the Front Desk and the Book

Problem: Stylists continually try to come behind the front desk to mark themselves off the book to leave early or reschedule their lunches.

Solution: The receptionist must professionally and authoritatively maintain control of the front desk and the book at all times in order to keep the salon running efficiently.

"When our stylists don't have a client booked after 5 P.M., they usually want to leave, even though we don't close until 6 P.M.," says Marlene Pisanti, salon manager and receptionist at London Hair in

Charleston, South Carolina. "I explain that the only way they are going to build their clientele is to wait for the next walk-in. The stylists who are always here are the ones making the most money, and I point them out as examples to help other stylists understand.

"The same goes for rescheduling lunches. We offer three price points and need someone here to accommodate walk-ins for each price point during all hours the salon is open. When they try to mark in the appointment book on their own, the salon can end up losing business." Marlene says that she handles this situation on her own most of the time, but every once in a while she has the topic raised at the salon's weekly staff meeting to keep it fresh in everyone's mind. "Once you let them behind the desk, you lose control of what's going on in the salon, and that should never happen," says Marlene.

Another important consideration when booking appointments is the addition of the computer to the salon reception desk. Receptionists in today's salons will eventually be using a basic salon program on a computer, which will enable the salon to keep better records and appointment schedules. The programs designed for salons are simple to use (user friendly) and lead the user step-by-step. The salon management may provide training when a computer is added to the salon, or you may wish to take a basic computer course in an inexpensive community college setting or even at free computer clinics that are held in public school continuing education courses. (See Figure 3-2.)

HANDLING STYLISTS' REQUESTS FOR SCHEDULING APPOINTMENTS

The ultimate responsibility of the receptionist when booking appointments is to retain the client for the salon and fulfill the client's needs as completely as she can; however, the receptionist must be able to handle special requests from stylists and consider these requests when booking appointments. For example: Joy is the manicurist/nail technician. She can do a set of nail tips with a wrap overlay in an hour-and-a-half, and a basic manicure in a half-hour. She has requested that the receptionist use this schedule of time to book her appointments, so that she will have ample time to serve her clients properly. If Mrs. Jones calls and requests a set of tips with wraps for Thursday at 8:30, and Joy has a client

Figure 3-2 A salon reception desk might use a computer as well as the appointment book for booking appointments.

at 9:30, the receptionist will have to suggest another time for the service, or suggest a basic manicure for that day and time, and another appointment for the tips/wraps on another day.

Another example of handling stylists' requests is that the receptionist should meet with all stylists and find out which services they perform and how much time each service requires. While Cathy may only need an hour for a hair-cut appointment, Mario may need to take an hour-and-a-half with each hair-cut client, because he is less experienced or simply works differently than Cathy. Failing to consider the staff's suggestions and requests for booking appointments could cause a backup in the flow of clients and may even affect the service a client receives. Therefore, it is very important that the receptionist and the staff meet and develop standards for booking client appointments.

Running Behind Schedule

Problem: A stylist is running late, and clients are getting nervous.
Solution: Your main objective in this case is to keep clients calm. When a client begins to get restless, first inform the late stylist that

the client is waiting and find out how long the stylist will need. Then explain the situation to the client, offer coffee and/or refreshments, and talk with the client about the appointment. This is a great opportunity for you to pre-sell retail products before the client even gets to the chair and to point out any new services your salon is offering. It will also give the client something else to think about. You might also want to take the client on a tour of the salon.

If the stylist is running more than 30 minutes late, you might want to offer a complimentary manicure, mini-facial, or deep conditioning treatment if any of those staff members are free. If not, offer the client the option to run errands and return or to re-book at another time. Chances are the client will opt to wait it out. If the stylist is running just a few minutes late, have another stylist or assistant begin the shampoo process, and make sure the service is extra relaxing. Letting clients know you care about their needs with a few kind words and your personal attention will usually head off any animosity and make you their favorite staff member too!

USING THE APPOINTMENT BOOK TO THE BEST ADVANTAGE

The appointment book is an important tool for the receptionist. If it is used properly, the staff will be booked fully and profitably, and the client flow will be smooth and pleasant.

Once you have a good idea of how long each service takes to perform, the receptionist should allocate the time profitably. For example, it would not be profitable to book Cathy with a 9:30 A.M. haircut (it takes her half an hour to perform this service) and then to book Cathy for another cut at 10:15 A.M. and another at 11:00 A.M. There would be fifteen minutes wasted between each haircut. Instead of wasting the time and opportunity to make more money, wouldn't it be better to ask clients to come in for their appointments at 9:30, 10:00, and 10:30? Then 11:00 would be free for a fourth haircut appointment, which could allow an extra client to be served, the stylist to earn more money, and the flow of clients to be steady, smooth, and hassle free!

Stopping Sick Time

Problem: Stylists who are not fully booked call in sick frequently.

Solution: At Markfrank Salon, salon coordinator Karen Ritt says that stylists who call in sick two or three times a month over a two-to-three-month period are told to take the week off—without pay. Clients are rescheduled with other stylists or re-booked for the following week—whichever is most convenient for them. Karen notes that it's usually only the lightly booked stylists who call in sick. "Some of my busiest stylists have never called in sick in the entire time they've worked here," she says. "They know how important it is to their clients, to the salon, and to their own earning potential that they are always here." When stylists have to take several days off—when they earn no money—they make the decision to either get serious about their careers or get out altogether. Either way, the client wins.

BOOKING CLIENT CONSULTATIONS

Often a new client or a client who is unsure of which service to get will require an appointment for a consultation. Many salons book new clients on certain days, with new stylists who have fewer demands on their time, since they have not yet built a steady following of clients. (See Figure 3-3.) Often these consultation appointments are booked on the first few days of the week, when the salon is not particularly busy. This special time (consultation) is an appointment to help the client become aware of the possibilities available and what the results, cost, and home maintenance will be. (See Figure 3-4.) For example: Mr. Jones is a new client with thinning hair. He wants to get a perm to help his hair look fuller, but he is unsure and anxious about the results. The receptionist books him with Jackie, who is new and has more time to spend with him than the older staff members who are more frequently requested. The receptionist has already talked to Jackie about the time required for the consultation. Jackie has told the receptionist that a 15-minute consultation is plenty of time for her to explain the service, show the client the possible results of different types of perms in a photo book, and explain the maintenance and cost involved. Since Jackie does not have any appointments for this Monday, the receptionist books Mr. Jones at

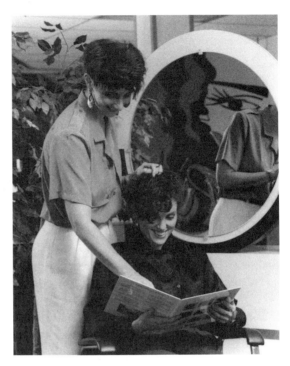

Figure 3-3 Scheduling client consultations requires a skilled receptionist adept at judging a stylist's time frame.

Figure 3-4 Often the receptionist will assist the stylist with a client consultation by suggesting a product to use for home maintenance.

9:00 for a consultation and 9:15 for a perm. It is usual to assume that Jackie will be able to help the client feel comfortable enough to have a perm following the consultation. There is usually not a fee for a consultation, because clients will have better results from any service they feel comfortable about purchasing. However, you should be guided by the policy for pricing in the salon in which you are employed.

No Shows? No Way!

At Markfrank, salon coordinator Karen Ritt has a strong policy for clients who are chronic no-shows or continually show up late: They can no longer make an appointment and can be served on a walk-in basis only. "Some clients regularly cancel three to five appointments during a week or just don't show up, and you have to draw the line somewhere or they end up disrupting the stylist's work flow and costing both the stylist and the salon too much money," says Karen. "At $35 a cut, that can mean a loss of $105 to $175 from one client's cancellations."

Clients are first given plenty of friendly warning, but if the problem persists, the line must be drawn. When the client finally does come in, Karen will pull her aside and nicely say, "I am sorry, Mrs. Smith, but you have continually canceled appointments or not shown up, and I must ask you not to book appointments over the phone any longer. We will be happy to serve you on a walk-in basis." Both the salon owner and the manager must support such a policy and not give in to the client for the policy to be effective.

SCHEDULING CHEMICAL SERVICES

Scheduling clients for chemical services is a difficult task. Many variables can cause the amount of time needed for a particular service to run over the allotted time. (See Figure 3-5.) For example: Ms. Leonora has color services every month. The usual time allotted for an appointment to have a color retouch is one hour, so when she calls, the receptionist books her appointment for 12:00 to 1:00. When the client actually arrives, her color is faded from a beach trip and a little discolored from chlorine pools, so the appointment goes over the scheduled time into the next client's appointment at 1:00. There are several ways to handle this problem.

Figure 3-5 Scheduling chemical services requires the receptionist to be aware of procedures and the stylists' work habits.

First, when the client booked the appointment, the receptionist could have asked her if there were any special needs for this appointment, or did Ms. Leonora feel this was a typical appointment for a color retouch. Was her hair in good shape, or did the client notice anything different? Second, the receptionist could have checked the client record card for notations from the stylist about her next appointment needs. The stylist may have told the receptionist to book extra time for Ms. Leonora the next time she called for an appointment, because her color was beginning to fade. Third, the stylist could have greeted the client, explained the special needs and time required, and re-booked the appointment for another day, or had the receptionist try to reach the client scheduled after Ms. Leonora and negotiate for a few moments' grace in a tight situation. When the receptionist and the staff work as a team, there are no problems too big to work around!

Scheduling chemical services is a challenging part of the receptionist's job. Each chemical service requires a different length of time to complete, and each stylist will need a specific length of time to perform each chemical service. Meet with the staff, become familiar with the chemical services offered and the basic principles involved in the process. Clients will ask you questions, and you will only be able to answer their concerns when you are informed.

The Client Needs More Time Than Was Booked

Problem: A client makes an appointment for hair color, and you book 30 minutes with her stylist. When she walks in, she needs a full foil highlight, which will take two hours, and her colorist is fully booked.

Solution: Never turn a client away. First, talk with her colorist to determine exactly how much time is available. Then, find another stylist to assist. Explain to the client that her regular colorist will place the foils in the front of her hair all around her face, while the "buddy" places the foils in the back under the supervision of the client's regular colorist. Let her know that not only will she have the attention of two wonderful stylists, she'll get in and out of the salon in half the time. This will also work for a permanent wave appointment.

The receptionist's main objective is to keep both the staff and the client calm while the problem is being corrected. Next time, the client might even request this "quick color" service.

REVIEW QUESTIONS

1. What are some ways to handle stylists' requests for scheduling?
2. What is a client consultation?
3. What must the receptionist take into consideration when booking a chemical service?

4 The Client and the Receptionist

LEARNING OBJECTIVES

After completing this chapter, you should be able to:

❶ Greet clients as they arrive and make them feel comfortable.
❷ Answer some client questions.
❸ Handle late arrival clients.
❹ Be able to route clients through the salon.
❺ Introduce new services to clients.
❻ Sell retail items to clients.
❼ Cash out clients and schedule appointments.
❽ Keep client records.

INTRODUCTION

The most important relationship the receptionist has is with the client. Greeting clients, taking care of their reception needs, and guiding them through services at the salon are important tasks. (See Figure 4-1.)

Often a new client feels uncomfortable on a first visit, or an established client requires more attention than usual. Sometimes a stylist may be running late and needs you to keep a client happy for a few minutes, and some clients have special needs and require extra attention every time they visit the salon. Whatever the client's needs are, you, as the receptionist, will be an asset to any salon if you are able to help the client have a comfortable and pleasant experience in the salon. (See Figure 4-2.)

Figure 4-1 Greet the client.

A large part of retail sales will depend on your salesmanship, and clients will rely on you to help them make choices of products and services.

The receptionist and the client have a special relationship, because no matter what stylist a client sees, the client will always be your client!

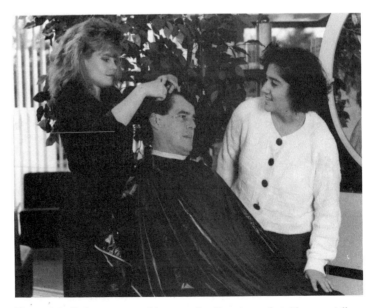

Figure 4-2 Follow up on making sure the client is comfortable, especially if this is a first-time client using a stylist you recommended.

Salon Tours Make Clients Feel Welcome

Many salons are introducing salon tours to make new clients feel welcome, and a receptionist is an ideal person to show clients around. The tour should cover every aspect of the salon, including the coat room, the coffee and soda machines, the shampoo area, the chemical services area, the nail- and skin-care areas, and the retail displays. During the tour, you can also talk about your salon's service and retail product guarantees. You will also want to tell the client that she is welcome to try any stylist at any time and encourage her to talk to you at any time if she has any questions.

During the tour, make sure the client meets the salon's owner, manager, artistic director, and the heads of any separate departments if they are available. Finally, introduce the client to her stylist, as well as anyone else she will see during her visit. Before launching salon tours, make sure you have a staff meeting to remind everyone to greet new clients warmly, say, "hi," and always offer to help them in any way. Many salons have new clients wear a different color cape so all of the staff members can take a team approach to helping new clients feel welcome.

GREETING CLIENTS

Greeting clients is a very important part of the receptionist's job. You are in a position to start clients off on a positive note that will carry them through the entire visit to the salon. Sometimes clients are uneasy about trying a new stylist or a new service. You will be able to make the client feel comfortable and relaxed by creating an environment that is relaxed and comfortable.

Greeting the client should always be done professionally. Always use the client's proper name. Never call the client by a first name or a nickname; this is not professional, and it could lead to a mistaken appointment. Use a polite greeting and then the client's full name. Small signs of respect, like using proper names and addressing the client on a pleasant note, can set the professional receptionist apart from the crowd.

Always acknowledge a client the moment he or she walks into the salon. Even if you are tied up with another client or a phone call, at least nod and smile at the client and make the client feel welcome!

CREATING A COMFORTABLE ENVIRONMENT

Be sure to answer the phone as soon as possible. The salon phone should never ring more than two or three times before you answer it. (Review phone reception in Chapter 2.)

In Chapter 1, we learned that the reception area must be neat and organized, as well as clean. It is also important that the waiting area be clean and pleasant. It should be a comfortable area for clients to sit and wait for their stylists. Some salons have coffee or beverages for clients, and some salons have videos to watch, which sell retail items or new services to clients as they wait for their appointments. Even the most modest salons will have an array of magazines and style books for clients to browse through. By greeting the client with a smile and a pleasant word, and helping the client get settled in the waiting area, the receptionist will be helping the client relax and prepare for the service. Whatever comforts are provided for the clients, it will be your responsibility to keep the waiting area clean, neat, and ready for the next client. Videos must be kept running, coffee brewing, and dirty cups cleared away. A messy waiting area will turn clients off, and they will not be able to relax. A comfortable waiting area is a must for a successful salon!

Clients with disabilities have special needs that the receptionist must meet. Wheelchairs must be able to fit through the doorways and aisles as well as in the waiting area, service areas, and rest rooms. The receptionist may be called upon to assist clients with disabilities in mobility as well as with moral support. Handicapped clients may require more moral support, and, as always, a helping hand and warm smile are always welcome.

ANSWERING PRELIMINARY QUESTIONS

Sometimes clients may not completely understand a service or the results that can be expected. To eliminate confusion, misunderstanding, and disappointment, it is helpful for the receptionist to answer preliminary questions that clients may have when booking appointments. For example: Ms. Cox books an appointment for a perm and haircut. While booking the appointment, Ms. Cox asks what brand of perm the salon uses and how long the service takes. This is basic information that a good receptionist will be able to share with the client. Make a list of the services offered in the salon; learn the brands of products used and the time required to achieve the desired results. Staff members should be able to supply any information you need, and there are always slow days in the salon that present a perfect time to observe services as the staff performs them. Ask questions and persevere!

Although you may seem overwhelmed at first, most of the information you will need to answer client questions is simple and easily learned. Some salons have books that you can borrow to train yourself on product knowledge and the basics of each service. Try every service you can, so that you will have first-hand knowledge of the procedure.

Problem Solving Turns Negatives into Positives

It's the nature of a service business that no matter how well you run your salon, you will get some complaints. When clients complain, the receptionist who steps in and takes control has the power to bring that client back. In fact, studies show that 70 percent of people will return to a business if their complaint is answered in their favor, and 98 percent will return if the complaint is solved in their favor and answered on the spot.

- Take over for the stylist about whom the client is complaining.
- Get the complaining client away from other clients—especially if the complaining is loud. Step away from the reception desk, preferably into a back room.
- Apologize. Show empathy for the client. Show that you care and understand how the client feels. Do not place blame on anyone. Look for a solution that will please the client.
- Ask the client to state the problem, and let the client tell the entire story.
- Repeat the problem back. Agree only with the client's perception of the situation. Use phrases such as "It sounds like you're not happy with the end result." By agreeing with the client's perception of the situation, you diffuse the anger and let the client know you want to help correct the problem.
- Ask, "Is there anything else you want to say?"
- Do not try to convince clients that they are wrong.
- Solve the problem beyond the client's expectations. Offer to have the service redone immediately. Do not try to re-book an appointment at a later date. The same goes if the client is to receive a refund—make sure it is taken care of immediately.

Your efforts will pay off with a happy client who can't even remember what the problem was. Instead, the client will concentrate on your nice way of handling the situation.

STYLE BOOKS

Style books are a necessary tool for a beauty salon. Clients may not be able to visualize styles that are explained verbally. By showing the client a picture of the style and explaining how to achieve that style, misunderstandings and disappointments can be avoided. Often the client does not have a specific style in mind, so browsing through style books can help a client make a choice. Style books should be kept current and in good repair. The receptionist should check the books often to be sure there are no tattered or loose pages.

The reception and waiting area is the perfect place to display style books; not only will the books be entertainment for waiting clients, but they may inspire the client to try something new, today! The receptionist should offer a style book to every client. (See Figure 4-3.)

Figure 4-3 Assist in providing a client with a style book.

HANDLING APPOINTMENT CONFLICTS AND LATE APPOINTMENTS

Even the most accurate receptionist will eventually be faced with an appointment conflict or a mistake. Often these conflicts will be caused by a client who arrives late for an appointment. This is a difficult situation and must be handled carefully, or a client may be offended. Example: Amber Nelson is a regular client. She is always at least 15 minutes late for her appointments. This causes her stylist (Gina) to run late and not be ready for the next client. The next client is upset because Gina is not ready when she arrives.

There are several ways to handle the late problem and the conflicting appointment problem. First, you may wish to explain to Mrs. Nelson that her business is important to the salon, but that when she is late Gina is sometimes rushed to serve her and runs over into the next client's appointment. Ask if it would be possible to book her appointments for the last appointment of the day, when time is a little more flexible.

Second, if Mrs. Nelson is always at least 15 minutes late, book her for 9:00, but tell her the appointment is at 8:45. When she arrives at 9:00, she will actually be on time.

The third choice is to explain that although you adore serving her, Mrs. Nelson has missed her appointment and you will have to reschedule her for another day/time. This is a rather drastic measure and should only be used when this is an ongoing problem or when there will not be a chance to be flexible for Mrs. Nelson. Be prepared to offer other stylists and appointments before you turn the client away; although the client is wrong, she may be upset at being turned away. Gentle tact is called for in this sensitive situation.

Mixups in dates or appointment times can happen. You may have given the client the wrong information, or the client may have misunderstood you. Your job as receptionist is to apologize for any inconvenience this error may have caused the client. Then talk to the staff member involved. Perhaps the stylist can squeeze the client in or offer another solution. Be pleasant and helpful, and try to help rectify a bad situation. Everyone makes mistakes, so relax and try to be more accurate in your appointment bookings. Always repeat the date and time for phone clients and write down appointments on a business card for appointments made in the salon.

WHEN STYLISTS RUN LATE

Sometimes the stylist will run behind schedule. Perhaps a service took longer than expected, or maybe a client was booked for one service, but needed another. (See Figure 4-4.) Also, new clients or clients who are difficult to please may require more time than is scheduled, and the stylist may run over the appointed time. This is when the receptionist really has a chance to shine! A well-trained receptionist will be able to greet the next client, explain the short wait ahead of her, and keep her occupied with style books, videos, retail items, small talk, and suggestions for new services. (See Figure 4-5.)

A sure way to involve the client in a conversation and pass the time is to ask the client about children, pets, or job. Everyone likes to talk about these things, and when a client is involved in a conversation about children, pets, or job, the time flies, and you have learned some valuable information about the client's

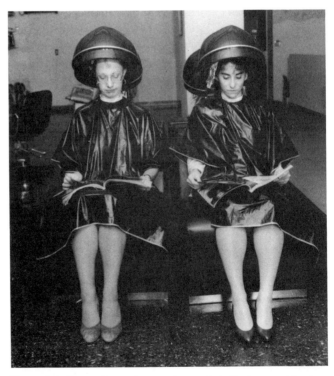

Figure 4-4 Remember to time services so that clients are not kept waiting.

Figure 4-5 Consider suggesting a manicure to a client who is waiting for a stylist who is behind schedule.

life-style. This information may help you later when you want to suggest a retail item or another service.

ROUTING THE CLIENT THROUGH THE SALON

Salon clients often see more than one staff member in a visit. Perhaps an assistant will shampoo the client, a stylist will cut the hair and style it, and a nail technician will manicure the nails or an esthetician will give the client a facial or a body spa treatment and massage. Your job, as the receptionist, is to fit all these appointments into a time frame that works well for the staff and the client. (See Figure 4-6.) Always begin with the longest service (the service that takes the longest to perform). Then book shorter services around it. For example: Book a perm client for 10:00. The nail technician can work on the client's manicure and pedicure while the perm is being done, and a leg wax can be done following the perm, at 12:00. This client will receive four services in less than two and a half hours, and as long as you have routed her properly through the salon area, she will be relaxed, refreshed, and ready to face the world when she leaves the salon. The staff members will perform the services, but only the receptionist will be able to route the client from staff member to staff member in an efficient and comfortable manner.

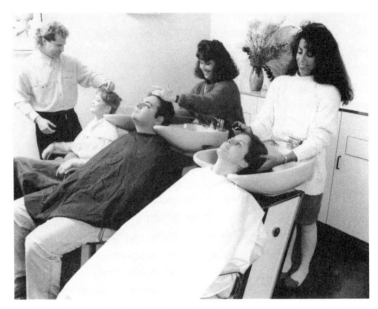

Figure 4-6 A well-trained receptionist will orchestrate the flow of services throughout a busy salon.

INTRODUCING CLIENTS TO ADDITIONAL SERVICES

As the receptionist, you will be able to introduce new and additional services to clients. Often you are alone with the client before the stylist is ready to begin the client's service. This is a perfect time to suggest other services to the client. (See Figure 4-7.) Other services could include

- Perms,
- Haircuts,
- Manicures,
- Pedicures,
- Nail art,
- Artificial nails,
- Waxing,
- Facials,
- Massage,
- Body treatments,
- Hair color,
- Relaxers,
- Makeup application.

Figure 4-7 Introduce clients to extra services, like hair ornaments to enhance a finished style.

Any service that the client is not already receiving can be an additional service. (See Figure 4-8.) First, survey the client's needs. Do not suggest a service that will be impractical for the client. Example: A new mother will not be interested in a fussy hairstyle or dragon-lady-length tips for hands that are caring for a newborn baby.

Do suggest a service that the client may need, but not be aware of. Example: A regular client who only has a haircut in

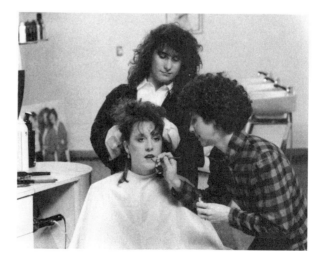

Figure 4-8 Suggest a makeup service to complement a client's new hairstyle.

your salon is beginning to get a little gray at the temples. Suggest a color rinse, and explain the process, cost, and show the client the results available. The client may not always agree with your suggestion, but you have created an interest and taken the opportunity to introduce a new service. If you make this a regular part of your reception duties, you will be able to help many clients become informed about the other services available to them in your salon. Perhaps a relative or a friend will even be referred when you begin to educate the clients about what services are available.

 Handling Clients with Head Lice

Problem: A hairdresser in your salon suspects a client has head lice. How do you handle it?

Solution: Say to your client, "Excuse me, Mrs. Jones, could I talk to you in the back room for a moment?" Escort her to a private, quiet part of the salon, then say, "John was just about to shampoo your hair and saw something that looked suspicious. It looks like lice. Have you been around any children who were at camp this summer or did you go camping yourself?" Most of the time the client will say, "Why, yes. My daughter Jennifer just returned from camp." If so, then continue, "I'm very sorry, but we cannot service you with this condition. It's against the law. Your local pharmacist can provide shampoo to solve the problem. As soon as your condition is cured, we'll be happy to offer you a complimentary shampoo. Here's a gift certificate for the service. Please come back soon."

CASHING OUT CLIENTS

When ringing up a client's bill, you will have the opportunity to sell the client retail items. (See Figure 4-9.) This is such an important part of the receptionist's responsibilities that the entire Chapter 7 will be devoted to retail sales. Cashing out clients is the process of adding up the client's bill and collecting payment for services rendered or products purchased. The receptionist must be accurate in all financial transactions. Chapter 5 will explain bookkeeping procedures for the receptionist. (See Figure 4-10.)

Figure 4-9   When a client is paying her bill, it is a good time to sell retail items.

Figure 4-10   The receptionist must be accurate in financial transactions.

Cashing Out with a Compliment

Imagine this scenario: Mrs. Gross has just had a half-day of beauty in your salon. She had her hair cut, colored, and styled, a facial, makeup application, manicure, and pedicure. She looks simply gorgeous and is thrilled with her look. She approaches the desk with a huge smile on her face. With her retail products, the total comes to more than $200. It's your job to tell her. "Clients get very excited about their new look, and because they are very emotional, they can become upset with the receptionist when they see the bill," says Kenneth Anders, owner of Kenneth's Design-group salons in Columbus, Ohio. "Therefore, it's always a good idea to comment on the new look right away and tell the client how great she looks as she approaches the desk. It can really help to soften the blow."

RE-BOOKING CLIENTS WHILE THEY ARE IN THE SALON

Many mistakes are avoided by re-booking clients while they are in the salon. When you re-book a client in person, you can give the client an appointment card with the time and date on it, as well as the stylist's name and the service to be given. This eliminates any chance for confusion and error. Also, clients who re-book while they are in the salon are almost certain to keep that appointment, while clients who do not re-book today may forget to call for an appointment or even be tempted to let the service go and try some home beauty preparations. Re-booking clients while they are in the salon helps generate business for the salon too! Re-booking helps the staff to plan their schedules, and the further in advance the stylist knows about the appointment, the more preparation and planning can be put into the client's total look of beauty. It is important to offer to re-book all salon clients before they leave the salon.

CLIENT RECORDS

Keeping client records is essential. Each stylist will make a notation on a client's record card after each visit. The receptionist should help the client make out the initial card on the first visit to the salon. It is also important to update the information frequently. The basic card could look something like this:

NAME _____

ADDRESS _____

CITY _____ STATE ___ ZIP _____

PHONE _____ WORKPHONE _____

ALLERGIES _____

MEDICAL PROBLEMS _____

DATE OF BIRTH _____

	Visit 1	Visit 2	Visit 3
DATE			
SERVICE			
FORMULA OR PRODUCT USED			
PRICE			
RETAIL ITEMS SUGGESTED			
RETAIL ITEMS PURCHASED			
SPECIAL NEEDS			
NOTATIONS			

Although the stylist will fill out most of the information, you should check to be sure there has been a card filled out and returned for every client, on every visit. Part of your responsibility will be to maintain a current file of client record cards and to pull the proper cards for every client who is booked for each day!

It is important that all client services be recorded. If the regular stylist is out sick, moves away, or quits the salon, there must be a record of every formula used on the client, so that someone else can continue the client's services in your salon. Also, if there is ever an allergy problem or a reaction to products, there must be a written record of services rendered.

Record cards can also be used to send client appointment reminder cards, birthday cards, letters for special promotions and sales, and get well cards. Clients appreciate the efforts and return to a salon where they are treated as special.

Handling an Unhappy Client

Problem: A client calls the day after her service to say she is very unhappy and never wants to return to that stylist again.

Solution: Since this client has already had a day to think about her problem before she called you, how you handle her problem and satisfy her need is even more critical to keeping her as a salon client, and dealing with her can be more challenging than dealing with the client who has still not left the salon.

Your best option is to apologize for how she feels, then book her with your salon owner (if the owner still works behind the chair) or your artistic director or senior stylist as soon as possible. Say, "Mrs. Jones, I am very sorry that you do not like your new color. Tilly, our salon owner, will want to see you right away so she can examine your hair and correct your problem personally. Of course, that service will be at no charge to you. Would you rather come in this afternoon at 3 or tomorrow morning at 10?"

When Mrs. Jones arrives, make sure she is greeted personally—at the door, if possible—escorted to Tilly's chair personally, and never left by herself or kept waiting. Ask her if she would like you to order a complimentary lunch if her appointment is near lunchtime. You might even want to give her a gift of a product or a gift certificate when she leaves, to bring her back. Finally, call her the next day to make sure she is still happy and to let her know again how much you care about her and appreciate her business. Let her know you are willing to do whatever it takes to keep it, too.

REVIEW QUESTIONS

1. Give an example of greeting a client properly.
2. What are some preliminary questions the client may ask the receptionist?
3. Define additional services.
4. What is a client record card?

5 Finances and Bookkeeping

C H A P T E R

LEARNING OBJECTIVES

After completing this chapter, you should be able to:

❶ Understand how to use the price list.
❷ Handle price objections from clients.
❸ Use basic accounting procedures for sales and credits.
❹ Understand how a cash register works.
❺ Be familiar with the basics of computers in salon accounting procedures.

INTRODUCTION

Handling money and performing basic bookkeeping tasks will be part of your responsibilities as the receptionist. In this chapter, we learn to properly cashier and keep records of financial transactions as well as how to use the price list to inform and serve clients. We will also gain basic knowledge of computer accounting. Many of the salon's financial transactions and records will be your responsibilities. Therefore it is essential that the well-trained receptionist be prepared to become proficient in these tasks. (See Figure 5-1.)

Overseeing 5 to 20 Separate Businesses at Once!

That's exactly what you will be doing when you work the front desk. "Anyone who works the desk must realize from the onset that each staff member is running his or her own separate business," says Karen Ritt, salon coordinator at Markfrank Salon. "When young stylists are first hired, I also take the responsibility for teaching them how to run their businesses." What does she emphasize?

- How to greet clients warmly and with a smile.
- How to leave the outside world outside the salon's door.
- How to purchase a day planner to keep track of clients, clients' services, and any important information that stylists need to remember.
- How to calculate how much their own commission check should be.
- How to walk clients to the desk and recommend the proper retail products at the end of the appointment.
- How to properly say good-bye to clients and invite them back.

"By reinforcing these points with new stylists, you're giving them a great support system and helping them develop strong professional habits that will continue throughout their careers," says Karen.

Figure 5-1 Keep accurate and neat business records.

PRICE LISTS

Every salon will have a price list. This list looks something like a menu in a restaurant. On the left side is a list of the services offered by the salon. On the right side is a price to coincide with the individual service. Here is an example:

Haircut	$20.00
Shampoo/Style	$15.00
Perms	$50.00, 70.00, 90.00
Facials	$40.00
Waxing	$20.00 & up
Manicures	$20.00
Tips/Wraps	$40.00/ 20.00 fill

Although the names of services may be different in your salon, and the prices will be different, this example shows the basic form of a price list. Note that several prices are listed for perms. This is because several perms are available in this salon. You, as receptionist, must be able to know the difference between perms and be able to explain the price difference. Meet with management and the staff and ask questions until you understand why each service is priced as it is and how to explain the difference. Until you understand the difference, you will be unable to assist clients with price information.

A price list is a basic necessity. Without it, staff members would charge different prices, and clients would be unable to decide which services they can afford. Even when the price list is used, there may be some confusion in pricing services. Because services are intangible, it is difficult to place an absolute price on each one. For example, the salon you work in may charge an extra ten dollars for perming long hair, because an extra bottle of solution is needed. Or there may be an extra charge for style haircuts compared with basic haircuts. Whatever the price difference, you must be able to explain it to clients and help alleviate any price objections or concerns they may have. You must also be able to help clients see the value in the pricing of each service. If you do not agree with prices, you will not be able to help clients feel comfortable with them. Communicate all price objections to management. You are in the best position to notice a trend in price objections, because you (as the receptionist) will be talking to all clients as you cash them out!

Explaining Your Salon's Price List

Many clients will have questions about your salon's price list, so you want to make sure you understand it thoroughly and can explain every service in detail. For example, if Mrs. Butterfield wants to know why single process color costs $35 while highlights are $80 and up, you will need to explain to her the difference in time, technique, and result. Remember, to her, it's all hair color. The same is true for explaining the difference between a $35 partial perm and a $100 spiral design wrap. The more details you can provide, the more interested your clients will be. As an added bonus, they will start thinking about the services, which gets their mind off the price altogether.

If you use different price structures for different stylists, you will also be prepared to explain the difference between a $20 haircut with Suzy and a $45 cut with Victoria, without making Suzy's work appear to have less quality. You can talk about how Victoria's technical knowledge, years in the business, and recent hairdressing championship awards have increased her demand, which means she can charge more.

Clients will also have questions about the price of professional products versus drugstore shampoos. To answer these questions as completely as possible, read and understand all of your manufacturers' product literature thoroughly. Then talk about your salon's guarantee and how salon products are developed for specific types of hair—permed, colored, highlighted, gray, thin, or unruly.

Remember, it pays to know about your salon's services and products at all times. The more information you can offer, the more confidence the client will have in you and your recommendations.

ACCOUNTING THE TOTAL PRICE OF SERVICES

Totaling clients' bills or accounting the prices of services is also a reception duty. Every client will have a sales check that will list the service rendered and a price. The sales check should have been started by the receptionist when the client arrived, or it may have been initiated by the first stylist to serve the client. All client sales slips will be a record of their purchases and services as well as the prices charged. The receptionist should check over the bill carefully to be sure that there are no errors in pricing or services listed. Be sure that no services that the client received are left off the list. Clients will point out over-pricing, but they may overlook a service that was not listed on their sales slip.

Sales slips may vary from salon to salon, but the basic sales slip will look something like this:

NAME _____

DATE _____

SERVICE _____ $ _____
SERVICE _____ $ _____
SERVICE _____ $ _____
SERVICE _____ $ _____

RETAIL PURCHASES _____ $ _____
RETAIL PURCHASES _____ $ _____

TOTAL _____

After writing the client's name and the date on it, as well as the requested services, route the sales slip through the salon with the client. Notice that there is a line for each service and price to be listed, as well as retail items bought. At the bottom there is a place to total the bill. Always double check the total with an adding machine or a calculator.

CREDITING FOR SERVICES AND RETAIL ITEMS

Sometimes clients will return merchandise or be unhappy with services received. Therefore you will have to refund their money or give them a credit. A credit is the opposite of a sale. Therefore, instead of adding it to the total of the client's bill, you will subtract it. Some salons do not issue refunds, only credits or exchanges. You must be guided by the policy of the salon you are employed in.

As a receptionist, you will be required to perform a variety of financial and bookkeeping services. The basic rule of thumb is: the smaller the salon, the more tasks you will be asked to perform. Such tasks include totaling tickets at the end of the day, closing the cash register either manually or by computer, closing the credit card machines, and even making bank deposits. You will want to brush up on your basic math skills and try to gain experience running an adding machine, calculator, and cash register. "There are so many different steps, it can become confusing if you don't keep everything straight," advises Karen Ritt, salon coordinator at Markfrank Salon. "Your best bet is to learn each task one step at a time. Learn everything you can about one task, concentrate on perfecting that task, and only when you are comfortable with that task should you move on to the next. This learning process will help you build a strong base of knowledge and develop your own level of professional confidence. "Just remember, it takes time to learn all about your new job. Be persistent, have patience, and don't get frustrated," says Karen.

CREDIT CARDS

Many businesses accept credit cards. The purpose of credit cards is to allow clients to make purchases without using cash. Some credit card users are accustomed to using a credit card instead of cash, enabling them to keep a record of monthly purchases.

Salons will charge the client's card with the purchases and collect the money from the credit card company. The company will in turn charge the client and send a bill. The salon pays a fee for the credit card service, but additional sales are often generated, because the client is able to purchase unplanned items and additional services. There are two basic types of credit cards. One is issued by a credit card company, and the client receives a bill each month for purchases made in the last 30 days. Some companies require the client to pay the bill in full each month, and some will allow the client to run a balance and pay a fee to finance the balance over a period of several months.

The second type of credit card is a debit card. The client establishes an account with the bank or company, and then the amount charged is deducted from the client's balance on hand. The use of debit cards is becoming more popular; therefore the receptionist must be trained by management to write sales and credits for charge clients.

Learning the Language of Computers

As more and more salons become computerized, having a general understanding of computers and how they work can help you as you enter the job market. In some cases the tasks will be as simple as working a computerized cash register or running name and address labels to do a mailing to clients. In other cases you'll literally be able to pull up the clients' entire histories. At Charles Penzone's The Grand Salon in Columbus, Ohio, 30 interlinked computer terminals tell the more than 20 receptionists everything about the client from the time of the current appointment to the preferred retail products. Receptionists immediately undergo computer training before they ever work the front desk. The bottom line, however, is still personality. Managers of even the most high-tech salons say they will forego computer experience in favor of a "people person" who smiles all day and puts service first.

USING A CASH REGISTER AND COMPUTER

Some salons have cash registers to ring up sales. Although each make or brand will have special features, the basic concept will be the same. There will be numbers printed on the buttons, and the receptionist must key in the prices and hit the total button. Some cash registers are sophisticated enough to have the services listed as well as prices programmed to match each service. By hitting a button the sale item will be listed with a price next to it. Salon management will train you to properly use the cash register.

As receptionist, it will be your duty to keep the cash drawer stocked with change. To set up the drawer with cash to start the day is called, "Setting up the bank." Be sure there is sufficient change and that you have bills in all denominations. Start a basic cash drawer (set up the bank) with twenty dollar bills, tens, fives, and many ones. Be sure you have quarters, nickels,

Figure 5-2 Computers are used in some salons for a variety of functions, such as keeping track of client information, appointments, and sales slips.

dimes, and pennies, too! It may also be your responsibility to go to the bank for change. Be guided by the management's policy for your salon. Always use caution when going for change. Conceal any money or bank deposit bags in a paper bag, and vary the times that you go to the bank. Never carry large sums of money alone; have another staff member accompany you if necessary.

Some salons have computers that keep track of client information, appointments, services, and sales slips. These basic computers are a wonderful time saver. They will even total the client's bill and keep a record of monthly and yearly purchases as well as a record of retail items bought. If the salon you are employed in has a computer, your work load will be reduced, and you will have more time to spend with clients. If you do not have any experience with computers, you may want to take a course or ask the management to help you understand the simple procedures involved. (See Figure 5-2.)

CHECK GUARANTEE PROCEDURES

Many businesses accept clients' personal checks. Unfortunately, not every check the client writes has money to back it up. If this happens, the check is returned to the salon unpaid, and in most cases the salon loses the money, a late fee, and a client. To avoid these losses, most businesses belong to a check guarantee program. The salon pays the check guarantee company a fee, and the company guarantees that the check will be honored. If the check is returned, the company buys it from you, and they have the responsibility to collect for it. Every check guarantee company follows different policies and procedures before they will guarantee the check. Be guided by management's instructions. The amount of money that businesses lose in bad checks annually is staggering, which is why many salons choose either not to accept checks or to use check guarantee companies.

Using Your Skills

Many of the skills that you learned during part-time and summer jobs during high school will be very important to your career as a successful salon receptionist. These are skills that you will want to highlight on your resume, especially for your first job after beauty school.

For example, at most jobs, from fast food restaurants to sales jobs, you learn how to run a cash register. You may even have responsibility for totaling the register at night, making bank deposits, or filing receipts. All of these are important skills that you will want to highlight.

Your customer service skills are also very important. Think about how you worked with that teenage girl to help her match just the right shoes for her prom dress. You must have brought in 20 pairs for her. Or consider how happy you kept the normally screaming Dougherty girls while their mother went to her corporate Christmas party. Those same skills can be applied to difficult clients.

In almost any job you also learn how to sell. Think about how every car visiting the drive-through window at the fast food restaurant is asked, "Would you like fries with your cheeseburger?" Most say, "Yes!" Now, you will turn those same skills into, "Would you like a manicure with your haircut today?"

When you apply for a receptionist position, experience counts, and any experience you have had is important.

REVIEW
QUESTIONS

1. What is a price list?
2. How do you calculate a credit on the client's bill?
3. Explain how a salon can accept a credit card for payment.
4. What is a check guarantee company?

6 Retail Sales

LEARNING OBJECTIVES

After completing this chapter, you should be able to:

❶ Explain the reasons for selling retail products in the salon.
❷ Understand what a product line is.
❸ Be able to suggest retail items.
❹ Understand suggestive selling, closing a sale, and how to handle sales objections.
❺ Understand how to keep a simple inventory.
❻ Be able to place a supply order.

INTRODUCTION

Selling retail items, or "retailing," is another aspect of the receptionist's responsibilities. Salons count on retail sales to help pay employee salaries and benefits as well as to defray the cost of staff training and expenses.

As the receptionist, you will come in contact with every client who comes in the salon. You may also have more time to explain the features and benefits of products to clients. Therefore, any salon in which you are employed will expect you to sell retail items. You must prepare yourself to become an expert salesperson and product expert.

There are five basic ingredients to a sale.

1. Know your products.
2. Know your client's needs and desires.

3. Show/suggest your products.
4. Answer client objections and concerns.
5. Close the sale.

In this chapter, we will expand on these five basic steps of selling.

Why Sell Retail Products?

Who wins when you sell retail products? Your clients, your salon, and you! In addition to adding to your salon's bottom line, there are very important reasons to sell retail products to your clients. Here are several:

First and foremost, professional beauty products help clients maintain the looks that their stylists created in the salon. A color enhancing shampoo helps keep color bright. A stiff spray keeps big hair big. Professional products can help keep your clients happy with their new looks between salon visits.

Next, clients who use proper professional products are walking advertisements for your salon throughout the city.

Finally, depending on your salon's policies and programs, selling retail products can help you earn extra bonuses or even prizes during special promotions.

KNOWING THE PRODUCT LINE

It is essential that the receptionist be familiar with the product lines that the salon carries. You must learn the purpose of every product and when to use it as well as how to use it. You must also be able to demonstrate the choice of sizes or colors that are available. (See Figure 6-1.) For example: Shampoo sells well in a salon. You must know which formula is for tinted hair, which is for scalps with dandruff, and which is for oily hair. (See Figure 6-2.) You must also know how many ounces are in each size (8 oz. or 16 oz.) and how much each size costs. Be prepared to help clients divide the cost by the number of ounces, so that they can tell which size is the best buy!

Figure 6-1 Read about your retail products.

The salon management and staff can help you learn all you need to know about the products, and you can read the labels and any literature that accompanies the products. Often sales representatives and manufacturers have product knowledge classes for salon staffs; be sure to attend and ask questions. (See Figure 6-3.)

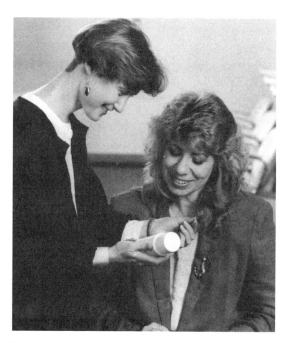

Figure 6-2 Know which product is best for a client's needs.

Figure 6-3 A salon manager or staff member can help a receptionist learn all about the products the salon sells.

TEAM SELLING

Interacting with salon staff to help clients make the correct choice of retail purchases is essential! Stylists will recommend products for their clients by suggesting products to them or writing down their recommendations on the client card. (See Chapter 4.) The receptionist should always try to consult the stylist for technical information needed to choose the correct retail items for their clients. For example: Mrs. Bradley has just had a perm and color. She has asked you which shampoo she should purchase, and you cannot decide if she needs shampoo for tinted hair or shampoo for permed hair. The best thing to do is to ask the stylist for a professional recommendation. If the stylist recommends the correct items and you spend time explaining the options to the client, the salon will succeed in making a retail sale every time!

Ring Up the Retail Sales

When stylists forget to suggest retail products, it's up to the receptionist to pick up the slack. Here are five suggestions from top selling receptionists:

- Know what products the stylist used on the client. There will be a *minimum* of three products—a shampoo, conditioner, and spray—for each client.
- Suggest the largest size first. Tell the client this size offers the best value. Also, it's easier to go down in price than up.
- Offer two products at once. For example, pair a shampoo and a conditioner or a spray and a gel.
- Like the products you are selling. Use the salon's products so you can speak from personal experience.
- Don't forget to suggest extra impulse items, such as makeup, lipstick, nail polish, and hand cream.

SUGGESTING RETAIL PRODUCTS

As a receptionist, you will be the perfect person to suggest retail items to clients.

You will have time alone with all clients either as they arrive or as they exit the salon. These would be perfect opportunities to suggest a pretty color lipstick or a new hair brush. The secret to selling retail products to a client is to truly believe the client needs the product! Don't be afraid to approach clients with suggestions. They will look to you, the professional receptionist, to suggest the items they will need to maintain their services once they get home! The client has made an investment in his or her appearance by purchasing a service; therefore, the client will welcome the idea of a product to help maintain a new style or chemical service.

Listening for Clues

Listening can be your greatest skill as a receptionist, and that's doubly true when it comes to selling retail products. Listen for clues from the moment clients walk in the door until the moment they leave, and they will almost always tell you what they need.

Here are some examples:

- Ms. Klein is complaining about her flyaway hair as she walks in the door. This is a clue that she needs a product to help her control it.

- Mrs. Barton is telling another client in the reception area that she is going to the Bahamas for two weeks, so you know to recommend a shampoo designed to keep her hair color from fading and a conditioner or spray containing sunscreen.
- If Mr. Sullivan mentions how great the styling gel his stylist used smells in his hair and doesn't have a bottle in his hand, you'll want to make sure that you hand him one to take home.
- You will want to listen for clues that offer the opportunity to suggest products, retail items, and gift certificates as gifts, too. If Mrs. Krakower says her daughter is turning 16 next week, recommend a day of beauty as the ultimate pampering present.

HOW TO SELL

We have discussed knowing your products and clients needs as well as suggesting items. However, in order to be successful in your suggestions you must also know the features and the benefits of a product. Features are the specific facts about the product. (See Figure 6-4.) Example: The features of a red plastic hair brush

Figure 6-4 Know the features and benefits of the products you sell.

for blow drying hair would be that it is red, it is made for blow drying hair, and it is plastic. The benefits of a product are what the product will do for the client. That same red hair brush has the following benefits: This brush will make blow drying easier; it is gentle on your hair and scalp; it is the type that the stylists all use.

Selling products can be as simple as this. The client walks up to the desk, and the receptionist, Gina, says, "Mrs. Jennings, I love your new hairstyle. We have just gotten in some new head bands that you may want to try; they really look cute (feature) with the new style you have chosen, and they help keep your hair out of your face (benefit) when you are looking down, reading. This is probably important to a librarian like you!" (Gina hands three head bands to the client.) Gina gave the client a reason to want the product, because she quoted a benefit and a feature that she knew would appeal to and help Mrs. Jennings.

You should also arrange displays that attract the client's attention. Clean, dust-free items that are well displayed and exciting are a boon to sales. If it is your responsibility to display retail items, and you are unsure of how to do it successfully, visit your favorite department store and borrow some ideas. They have professional display staffs who can really promote retail items with display ideas—especially at holidays. Also observe displays in discount stores and retail store windows.

CLIENT OBJECTIONS

Often, no matter how good you are at suggesting products, stating benefits and features, or displaying items, clients will have objections or concerns. Sometimes the client will have questions like, "Does it come in a larger size? Does it come in pink? How often should I use this?" These simple questions create a conversation about the product, and as the client has shown an interest in it, you will be able to sell it as you answer the questions.

Sometimes clients will have a concern (Will I be able to do this at home?) or even an objection (It's too expensive!). Do not be afraid to deal with client concerns or objections. Draw upon the product knowledge that you have learned, answer each concern and objection honestly, and be pleasant while you are doing it! Suggest an option or an alternative product when the client's objections are valid. Here is an example of a client objection: "I

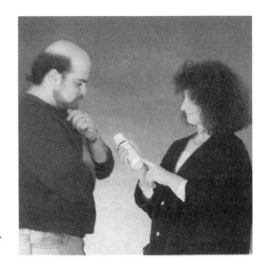

Figure 6-5 Be ready to answer a client's questions about your products.

cannot use hair spray; it makes my scalp itch." The receptionist could reply: "You may want to try this new hair spray; it's designed for people who have itchy scalp problems." After suggesting an alternative, back off and allow the client room to accept or reject the substitute that you suggested. Remember, be helpful, cheerful, and pleasant as you make suggestions and answer objections. (See Figure 6-5.)

CLOSING THE SALE

There are several ways to close a sale. After you have created the interest, suggested a product, listed benefits and features, and answered objections and concerns, it is time to close the sale. This means to finalize or wrap up the sale. (See Figure 6-6.) You can use closing statements like:

- Will this be a cash or charge sale?
- Would you like the large or small size today?
- Shall I gift wrap this for you?
- Would you like to take one or two bottles today?

Notice that you never ask if the client would like to buy it. Ask a question that helps the client to decide to take it, by choosing a size, color, number of items, gift wrapping, or whether the client will be charging the purchase. Asking if the client will buy it can end up with a "no" answer, so try to use questions that give the client a choice, but don't ask if the client will buy.

Figure 6-6 When a client decides to buy a product or service, you have closed the sale.

 Five Steps to Super Sales

Michael Cole, president of Salon Development Corporation, a salon industry education company based in St. Paul, Minnesota, teaches five steps for increasing retail sales. They are:

1. Bonding: Always strive to create a good first impression in person or on the phone. In person, greet the client, make the client feel comfortable, offer a magazine and coffee, water, or a soda. Be courteous and caring.
2. Discovery: Learn to listen to cues from clients. Almost any statement a client makes about hair, skin, nails, or life-style provides a selling opportunity for you.
3. Advising: Suggest products that solve the client's problems or make a beauty routine easier.
4. Closing: When packaging the client's products, always ask, "Is one enough?" or "Are you close to running out of any other products?"
5. Follow-up: Offer free samples of your newest products that clients can take home and try for themselves. Include a brochure or flyer from the manufacturer. Give the client three days, then call to follow up and see if the client liked the new product. You can offer to "special order" one and hold it at the desk until the next time the client comes in.

INVENTORY CONTROL

Often it is the receptionist's responsibility to keep track of inventory. Inventory is the number of items or stock the salon has on hand. Keeping inventory is simple. Make a list of products and include how many you have of each item, size, and color next to the item.

Example:

Size:	Item:	Number on hand:
8 oz.	dandruff shampoo	2
16 oz.	dandruff shampoo	16

By comparing this list (inventory) to the amount of products on hand last month, the management will be able to decide how many items were sold and which items to reorder. It is important to do the inventory accurately. Slow selling items may be eliminated or placed on sale, and new items can be ordered, all based on the information you provide in the inventory.

HOW TO ORDER PRODUCTS

Often the receptionist will help with ordering products. The basic rule for re-ordering is to subtract what the salon has sold from what was originally purchased. When you know how many you have used and how fast your salon sold it, you can decide which items should be eliminated, re-ordered, or replaced. After you decide what to order, check to see in what quantity it is available. Some items are only sold in cases of 8, 12, or 24 items. A slow-selling item that is sold only in cases of 24 may be a good prospect for replacing with a new, more popular, item that is available in cases of 8. Consult management before changing brands or manufacturers. Orders are placed on the phone, at the beauty supply store, or through a salesperson who visits the salon. You, as the receptionist, will probably deal with all the sales representatives, because either staff members and managers will be unable to leave clients or you will have the ordering responsibility and know what the salon needs from your inventory and order plans.

Stocking Up

Most salons have three or four products that literally fly off the shelves. These are usually the stylists' favorite products, too. That's great for the bottom line, but bad if you can't keep enough of the product in stock. Every minute that a product is "on order" can equal dollars lost.

To control inventory, keep a tally of how many of the favorites you sell each day, and then each week for a month to determine your average sales. Then place your order to accommodate your busiest period. You can also ask your distributor sales consultant to help you estimate how much product you will need to order. Or get creative. When clients book their appointments, ask if they will need to restock on their favorite products and let them "place an order." That will give you an idea of how many guaranteed sales you'll have that week. Remember, keep your shelves fully stocked. Clients will buy what's out and ready for them.

REVIEW QUESTIONS

1. What are the five basic steps of selling?
2. What are the features and the benefits of a product?
3. What are client objections?
4. How do you close a sale?

7 Marketing and Advertising

LEARNING OBJECTIVES

After completing this chapter, you should be able to:

❶ Observe business trends to direct ads and promotions.

❷ Conduct informal polling and research as you serve clients.

❸ Assist with client questionnaires.

❹ Understand the use of coupons.

❺ Be able to create in-salon displays.

❻ Assist with salon promotions.

INTRODUCTION

The salon receptionist is a vital part of all salon advertising and promotions. The receptionist must be able to poll clients for personal opinions and preferences, as well as keep track of trends in services and products most often requested. The receptionist may even help keep track of ads and the results from the ads. The receptionist is the key to successful promotions and advertising in the salon!

Your High-Impact Reception Area

Your reception area creates the first impression a client receives of your salon. It tells the client right away if she can expect the salon to be neat, clean, professional, fashion forward, and service-oriented just by looking at your magazines, ashtrays, posters, and product displays. As a receptionist, creating and maintaining this area will probably fall under your job description. Here are a few pointers to help you increase your retail and service profits through your reception area:

- Select magazines that keep clients focused on their hair, makeup, and nails. Include a variety for each type of client you serve. Make sure magazines are current, arranged neatly, and kept in good condition. Using plastic magazine covers is always a good bet.
- Create an easily accessible reading shelf for your retail product brochures, salon newsletter, and fliers describing current and upcoming salon activities and promotions.
- Display retail products in buyer-friendly arrangements. Include plenty of sample sizes and open bottles so clients can see, touch, and smell the actual products. Most important: tidy and dust these displays every two to three days. Nothing turns off clients more than dusty shelves. Surveys show that the number one reason a client leaves a salon is lack of cleanliness.
- Professionally post current styles created by your staff members, as well as posters from your product manufacturers and pages from magazines.
- Make sure your signs, shelf talkers, and fliers are professionally produced so they visually represent your image to your clients.

When in doubt about your reception area, go outside and enter the salon like a client. Ask yourself, "What message does this area convey to me?"

RECEPTIONIST'S OBSERVATIONS

The receptionist must be able to observe trends in business. By recording how many clients request a certain stylist or service, the management will be able to judge which stylists are doing well and which may need more promotion or training, as well as which services are requested and which need to be promoted more. You can also keep track of retail sales so that sales trends can be monitored.

The Client Card

Most salons keep a variety of information on their clients either on cards in a file drawer or in a computer file. This information is used to do direct mail programs, send clients thank-you notes for referring new clients, mail birthday cards, or to send out newsletters. This information can also be used to track where most of your clients live and work, what types of services they currently receive, and what types of new services they would like to try.

This information is obtained by the receptionist during the client's first visit by having the client fill out an information sheet. In fact, the receptionist will want to ask new clients to come in about 10 to 15 minutes early to provide this information. On the cards, the client will fill in the name, address, and telephone numbers for home and work. Next, ask questions about previous salon experiences. Provide boxes so a client can check off all previously tried services, then leave spaces where you ask for comments on positive and negative impressions about those experiences.

You will also want to ask questions such as, "How often do you get your hair cut?" "How often do you get your hair permed?" and "How often do you get your hair colored?" Do the same for other services your salon offers, including manicures, pedicures, and skin-care services. In addition, ask what products the client uses at home. Finally, ask how many family members live with the client so that you can direct pertinent promotions to the entire family.

It's best to have cards or forms professionally printed. When possible, provide check boxes for information to make filling out the forms as easy as possible.

Keeping track of requested items, services, and stylists can be as simple as marking slash marks next to the name:

Date: 1-5
Perms requested: ЖЖ ЖЖ
Color requested: //

or

Date: 1-8
requests for Janie: ЖЖ ЖЖ ЖЖ ЖЖ
requests for Sam: ///

or

Hair spray sales during sale: ☐ ☐ ☐

Keeping track of promotions and ads can also be part of the receptionist's observations. If the salon has placed an ad in a newspaper, a magazine, or on the radio or television, and management wants to determine how many responses there were to the ad, the receptionist may be required to track the ad. A simple form may be used to record results:

Date of Ad: June 14   Today's Date: June 21

(A)	(B)	(C)
Calls	Walk-ins	Bookings
☐ ☐	///	☐ ☐ ///

You will notice that by making slash marks every time a client called about the ad (A), walked in to the salon because of the ad (B), or booked an appointment because of the ad (C), the actual results of the ad are recorded. Management can then total the week's results and decide if the ad was worth the money spent to attract new clients or if another method of sales promotion should be considered. Management can also tell if clients who call because of the ad are booking appointments or not. Perhaps the ad was not clear and needs to be revised. Or the receptionist is not able to complete or close the phone sale of an appointment. (Chapters 2 and 7 discuss closing sales.) Since advertising can be very costly, it is essential that the receptionist keep accurate records when tracking results.

INFORMAL POLLING OR RESEARCH

Sometimes the receptionist will be called upon to research client opinions or poll clients. By using a few standard questions with clients and keeping track of the results, management will have informal results upon which they may base services and retail stock offered. Example: A new service (waxing) is being offered in the salon. As receptionist, Janie is required to ask clients if they are aware of the new service and write down the results. Then she will explain the new service to each client. Janie can help to introduce the service and generate sales at the same time.

The same questioning method could be used to ask clients which services they would like to see added to the menu. The results of this informal poll could institute a new service for the salon to offer and create a job opening for a new stylist or technician. The receptionist is in the best position to poll and survey clients.

Client Newsletters

Newsletters can be very effective, all-encompassing marketing, sales, and public relations tools all wrapped into one. The reception desk can be a key center for gathering and tracking information to include in the newsletter.

Popular newsletter pieces include new services and products offered by the salon, new staff members, and current promotions offered by the salon. You will also want to include information about awards won by your salon or individual staff members. Many salon newsletters also include personal information about the staff, such as births, marriages, and other important milestones of interest to clients. You might also want to include service articles, such as new trends in beauty or tips on how clients can style their hair into the most current looks using products sold in your salon.

The beauty of a newsletter is that clients will read it, they will appreciate your keeping them informed, and it is an inexpensive way to remind them about how great you are!

CLIENT QUESTIONNAIRES

Often management will want a survey or questionnaire to be completed by all the clients. The receptionist will offer each client a questionnaire on a clip board and, if needed, assist the client in filling it out. A questionnaire is a series of questions that give management an objective opinion of the clients' impressions and observations as well as desires. The receptionist would keep the questionnaires, and the management would use them to help the business grow! The following is an example of a salon questionnaire.

Ventura's Institute of Nail Technology
123 Fourth Street
New York, NY 10016

1. How often do you visit a beauty salon?
2. Which services do you now receive?
3. Which services would you like to have more information on?
4. How happy are you with the services you now receive in our salon?
5. How can our nail technicians serve you better?
6. Which products would you like to see our salon carry?
7. Which products are you using for your home care of nails, hands, and feet?

Thank you for your opinions and your suggestions! You are the reason our salon is in business, and your desires and concerns are our first concern!!

USING COUPONS AND OTHER SPECIAL OFFERS

Often management will place a coupon in an ad or a flier. This will enable them to track how many new clients responded to the ad. Also, clients tend to keep an ad that has a coupon on it for a longer period of time than if there was not a coupon on it! As a receptionist, you will be required to help the client use coupons correctly. For example: a coupon was in the salon's ad this week. It offers 20 percent off a perm, with STYLISTS WHO ARE CHOSEN ESPECIALLY FOR THIS PROMOTION. (This means that all the stylists are not participating in this sale. The purpose of the sale is to help build up business for new stylists who are not always booked up.)

The receptionist must make sure that all clients who present the coupon are aware that their own stylists may not be participating in this sale. Therefore they may want to forgo the coupon and stay with their usual stylist. Inform clients that customer appreciation day sales are being planned for them or that the expertise and good results they have come to enjoy with their usual stylist is an unbeatable value too.

Sometimes a coupon may have an expiration date or limited time offer. Other coupons will be for a discount on one item when the client purchases another item listed. There are many types of coupons, and you must redeem them carefully. Clients may be offended if they are unable to use a coupon, or if a coupon is redeemed for the wrong stylist or service, the salon may lose money. Be sure to have management explain all coupons and special promotions before they are sent out!

Beyond the Client Questionnaire—The Client Survey

Before your salon launches any new service, you will need to know if your clients will purchase the new service on a regular basis. The best way to do that is to launch a market research effort. What is market research? It is the process you use to gather information to help guide your marketing decision.

One of the easiest and least expensive market research methods is the client questionnaire. As the receptionist, you will play a key role in ensuring that the surveys are completed thoroughly and provide the information that the salon owner needs to make a decision.

Here are five tips for conducting a successful survey:

- Keep it short and simple, and make sure it takes only a few minutes to fill out.
- Survey a large enough percentage of your clients to gauge accurate results.
- Ask a wide cross section of clients of all ages and life-styles.
- Send at least 50 percent of your surveys by mail.
- Always thank clients with small gifts, such as samples or retail products, and follow with thank-you notes for taking the time to help you.

DISPLAYS

Helping the salon market products and services may also include setting up and maintaining displays. (See Figure 7-1.) It is fun to create displays with products, especially at holiday times. Pretty fabrics and baskets with tissue paper can be used to create attractive displays and gift baskets. Mirrors and stuffed animals as well as statues and ornaments are nice additions, too! There are endless ideas for retail displays—just visit any mall and window shop! You will see great ideas on color, style, and themes for displays. Even shelves with retail items lined up can be kept neat,

Figure 7-1 Help the salon by setting up and maintaining retail displays.

orderly, and attractive! Keep some samples and open bottles as testers. (Testers are open bottles for clients to see, feel, touch, smell, and try.) With a little practice you can create a display that will really draw attention to products. Do not forget to place displays in the windows—they really draw attention! (Caution— sunlight changes products, and some products are flammable, so use empty containers in windows!)

IMPULSE BUYING

When you consider retail displays, think about creating an impulse sale area. Clients will buy small, necessity items that are displayed at the register. Think about the register areas at supermarkets or convenience stores. There are many useful items that are inexpensive and are purchased on impulse. (An impulse is a sudden inclination to act.) Small or inexpensive items can be placed in baskets or jars or on displays at the register area in the salon. Impulse items can account for many retail sales, especially as last minute gift ideas at holiday times. Gift wrap a few, and have them ready to go home with clients!

Displays for services can be fun to create. Posters and photos, wigs, and hair samples are great visuals. Remember, a picture is worth a thousand words! Telling a client about the new shade of blonde highlights your salon is offering is nice, but having hair samples that can be held up to the hair to see the contrast will close the sale! Of course, the best visual aid or display you have for services is your own well-groomed hair, nails, and makeup. You are the salon's best advertisement and display!

Manufacturers of perms, colors, and relaxers will provide you with photos of new services. They depend on your success for their success, so they will usually help you promote the service. They will even be able to offer co-op advertising money on occasion. (This means that when you advertise their products in connection with a service, they will help your salon pay for the ad.) Sometimes manufacturers will provide samples to help introduce new services or products, too.

Being creative and helping the staff find new ways to promote services will help make your job as receptionist more rewarding and fun.

On occasion, management will run retail or service sales contests for the staff. Sometimes you will be asked to keep track of the results, just as you keep track of ad results. Make a list of the stylists' names and make slashes every time they sell the item or service involved. These contests create excitement and the spirit of competition, inspire sales, and generate money. Every time a promotion is successful, you can feel the pride of knowing that you were the quarterback that lead the team to the touchdown! Without the receptionist to help with promotions, sales, and advertising and to keep track of the results, advertising would be a guessing game and a very costly trial-and-error expense for the salon. The receptionist is the first and last word in salon promotion.

One Final—But Very Important—Tip

No matter what other skills you develop and knowledge you gain from your schooling and experience, this one final tip might hold the key to your success as a top receptionist: From day one, wear good support hose and comfortable shoes. If you don't, you are likely to be very uncomfortable by the middle of the day—especially if you stand at the desk all day—and it will show on your face, in your voice, and in your overall attitude.

REVIEW QUESTIONS

1. What is a questionnaire?
2. What is meant by tracking results?
3. What are some ideas you have for creating a retail display for Independence Day?
4. Why would a salon use a coupon in an ad?

Projects

1. Write an essay telling why you want to become a receptionist and what you feel you will gain from this occupation. Include a description of an efficient receptionist and explain how a receptionist maintains salon culture. Tell what skills you possess that will enable you to maintain salon culture.

2. Practice booking appointments. Pretend there is a client on the phone, and write down a phone message for your manager. The message should mention that a client called to make an appointment but wanted to speak to the manager personally. The client's name was Mrs. Starr, phone number 555-1212. Fill out the phone message form on the following page with the pertinent information.

3. The class should divide into two teams for the following exercise. Team A will be the receptionist who answers the phone; Team B will pretend to be the client calling from home. Team B members will pretend to book or change an existing appointment (as a client would), and Team A will make or change the appointment (as a receptionist would). Take turns coming to the front of the class, in pairs, and role playing. The instructor will supervise each pair of students, and the class can discuss what they thought worked well or could have been done differently. Use the appointment sheet provided here as a worksheet for filling in appointments. If time allows, reverse the teams so that everyone has a chance to be the receptionist.

```
┌─────────────────────────────────────────────┐
│ To _____  ☐ URGENT         │
│                                        A.M.   │
│ Date _____ Time_____       P.M.   │
│                                               │
│        WHILE YOU WERE OUT                     │
│                                               │
│ From_____  │
│ Of _____ │
│ Phone _____ │
│       Area Code      Number      Ext.         │
│ Telephoned      ☐     Please call       ☐     │
│ Came to see you ☐     Wants to see you  ☐     │
│ Returned your call ☐  Will call again   ☐     │
│ Message _____ │
│ _____  │
│ _____  │
│ _____  │
│ _____  │
│ _____ Signed _____  │
│ Notes _____ │
│ _____  │
│ _____  │
│ _____  │
└─────────────────────────────────────────────┘
```

4. Use a sheet of appointment book paper to book the following appointments. (This assignment should be done in class, with the instructor explaining how, when, and where to write the appointments. The teacher may wish to use a chalkboard or overhead projector with transparencies to illustrate the examples.)

Monday, January 15, 1993

Stylist: Mary
Appointments: 10:00 A.M.—Haircut for Mr. Smith, 555-1314. 12:00 P.M.—Perm for Mike Woods, 555-6666. 2:00 P.M.—Relaxer for Ms. Kirkland, 555-1478. 5:00 P.M.—Haircut for J. Jones, 555-1111.

Stylist: John
Appointments: 4:00 P.M.—Haircut for Ms. Johnson, 555-1212.

Manicurist: Susan
Appointments: 10:00 A.M.—Manicure for Mr. Small, 555-1999. 12:00 P.M.—Manicure for Mrs. Lome, 555-1543. 4:00 P.M.—Nail Wrap for Ms. Louis, 555-7778.

APPOINTMENT SHEET

DATE

STYLIST'S NAME	STYLIST'S NAME	STYLIST'S NAME	STYLIST'S NAME	STYLIST'S NAME
8:30	8:30	8:30	8:30	8:30
9:00	9:00	9:00	9:00	9:00
9:15	9:15	9:15	9:15	9:15
9:30	9:30	9:30	9:30	9:30
9:45	9:45	9:45	9:45	9:45
10:00	10:00	10:00	10:00	10:00
10:15	10:15	10:15	10:15	10:15
10:30	10:30	10:30	10:30	10:30
10:45	10:45	10:45	10:45	10:45
11:00	11:00	11:00	11:00	11:00
11:15	11:15	11:15	11:15	11:15
11:30	11:30	11:30	11:30	11:30
11:45	11:45	11:45	11:45	11:45
12:00	12:00	12:00	12:00	12:00
12:15	12:15	12:15	12:15	12:15
12:30	12:30	12:30	12:30	12:30
12:45	12:45	12:45	12:45	12:45
1:00	1:00	1:00	1:00	1:00
1:15	1:15	1:15	1:15	1:15
1:30	1:30	1:30	1:30	1:30
1:45	1:45	1:45	1:45	1:45
2:00	2:00	2:00	2:00	2:00
2:15	2:15	2:15	2:15	2:15
2:30	2:30	2:30	2:30	2:30
2:45	2:45	2:45	2:45	2:45
3:00	3:00	3:00	3:00	3:00
3:15	3:15	3:15	3:15	3:15
3:30	3:30	3:30	3:30	3:30
3:45	3:45	3:45	3:45	3:45
4:00	4:00	4:00	4:00	4:00
4:15	4:15	4:15	4:15	4:15
4:30	4:30	4:30	4:30	4:30
4:45	4:45	4:45	4:45	4:45
5:00	5:00	5:00	5:00	5:00
5:15	5:15	5:15	5:15	5:15
5:30	5:30	5:30	5:30	5:30
5:45	5:45	5:45	5:45	5:45
6:00	6:00	6:00	6:00	6:00
6:15	6:15	6:15	6:15	6:15
6:30	6:30	6:30	6:30	6:30
6:45	6:45	6:45	6:45	6:45
7:00	7:00	7:00	7:00	7:00
7:15	7:15	7:15	7:15	7:15
7:30	7:30	7:30	7:30	7:30
7:45	7:45	7:45	7:45	7:45
8:00	8:00	8:00	8:00	8:00
8:15	8:15	8:15	8:15	8:15
8:30	8:30	8:30	8:30	8:30
8:45	8:45	8:45	8:45	8:45
9:00	9:00	9:00	9:00	9:00

An alternative exercise would be to break the class into two teams and allow each person to come up to the desk and book an appointment for a person on the opposite team. Use a chalkboard or overhead projector with transparencies so that all students can see the appointment and discuss the reasoning.

5. Design a pricelist for a salon. List at least ten services and the prices for each service. Be sure prices and services are realistic. You may wish to use the following form to organize your pricelist.

(SALON NAME)

SERVICES: PRICE:

_____
_____
_____
_____
_____
_____
_____
_____
_____
_____
_____

6. Visit a local drugstore or department store. Choose one line of products, and write down the name of each item in it and a benefit of each product. For example:

APPLE PECTIN HAIR PRODUCTS

1. Shampoo—gently cleans scalp and hair.
2. Conditioner—leaves hair tangle free and shining.
3. Setting gel—helps hold hair in a set.
4. Hair spray—holds style in place for hours.

Prepare a sales presentation on this line of products. Be ready to share your presentation with your classmates.

Answers to Review Questions

Chapter 1
1. A professional image
2. That the salon cares about their needs and is prepared to provide great service
3. Because you never get a second chance to make a first impression
4. A well-kept reception area, a good personal appearance, a pleasing tone of voice, a willingness to be a team worker, and a genuine smile
5. Personal opinion answer

Chapter 2
1. command
2. make; cancel
3. The benefits of a product
4. Feelings
5. Talk to the client calmly, and suggest an alternative to canceling her appointment. Suggest another service, and encourage her with your own personal experiences.

Chapter 3
1. The receptionist can handle stylist requests for scheduling appointments by meeting with stylists, finding out their requirements for each service, and making a list to keep next to the appointment book.
2. Client consultations are appointments in which the stylist meets with the client to discuss the possibilities of the service desired, the results available, and the cost and maintenance involved.

3. When booking a chemical service appointment, the receptionist must consider which stylists perform this service, how long the service takes to perform, and the basic mechanics of the actual service.

Chapter 4
1. Greeting a client properly may include smiling, calling the client by the proper name, and being helpful and pleasant.
2. Some preliminary questions the client may ask you are
How much does it cost?
How long does it take to do?
How long does it last?
How is it done?
3. Additional services are any services the client is not already having.
4. Client record cards list the client's personal information, the dates of service and the services performed, the formulas, and the brands of products used. It may also list suggested retail items and services as well as money spent.

Chapter 5
1. A price list is a list of services that the salon offers and the price of each service. Retail items may also be listed on a price list.
2. A credit on a client's bill is a refund or a return of money for a service the client was unhappy with or a retail item that was returned. A credit is the opposite of a sale.
3. A salon accepts credit cards for payment from clients. The salon pays the credit card company a fee, and the credit card company pays the client's bill and then collects the money directly from the client.
4. A check guarantee company charges the salon a fee to guarantee that every check will be honored by the bank, or the check company will buy it from the salon and collect it themselves.

Chapter 6
1. The five steps to selling are: know your products, know the client's needs and desires, show/suggest products, answer objections/concerns, and close the sale.
2. The features of a product are the description of the product. The benefits of a product are what the product does for the client.
3. Client objections are concerns or reasons the client doesn't want to make the purchase.

4. You can close a sale by asking the client to choose between sizes, styles, colors, quantity of items they would like to take, if gift wrap is needed, or how they would like to pay (cash or charge).

Chapter 7

1. A questionnaire is a form that management may ask the receptionist to help clients fill out. It asks the client for opinions, desires, and concerns, as well as for input for future sales, services, and items.
2. Tracking results is the method that the receptionist may use to keep track of results from an ad or sale. It can be as simple as making slash marks on a paper or collecting coupons.
3. Ideas or a retail display for Independence Day can be varied! The use of red, white, and blue or small flags could be one plan. Sparkler and firework look-alikes could be used too. The possibilities are limited only by your imagination!
4. Salons include coupons in their ads because it helps them keep track of how many clients came in because of the ad, and because clients tend to keep ads that have coupons in them.